Unit Sizes in the Late Roman Army

Terence Coello

BAR International Series 645
1996

Published in 2016 by
BAR Publishing, Oxford

BAR International Series 645

Unit Sizes in the Late Roman Army

ISBN 978 0 86054 830 0

© T Coello and the Publisher 1996

Volume editor: Rajka Makjanić

The author's moral rights under the 1988 UK Copyright,
Designs and Patents Act are hereby expressly asserted.

All rights reserved. No part of this work may be copied, reproduced, stored,
sold, distributed, scanned, saved in any form of digital format or transmitted
in any form digitally, without the written permission of the Publisher.

BAR Publishing is the trading name of British Archaeological Reports (Oxford) Ltd.
British Archaeological Reports was first incorporated in 1974 to publish the BAR
Series, International and British. In 1992 Hadrian Books Ltd became part of the BAR
group. This volume was originally published by Tempvs Reparatvm in conjunction
with British Archaeological Reports (Oxford) Ltd / Hadrian Books Ltd, the Series
principal publisher, in 1996. This present volume is published by BAR Publishing,
2016.

Printed in England

PUBLISHING

BAR titles are available from:

        BAR Publishing
        122 Banbury Rd, Oxford, OX2 7BP, UK
EMAIL   info@barpublishing.com
PHONE +44 (0)1865 310431
FAX   +44 (0)1865 316916
        www.barpublishing.com

CONTENTS

	Page
Introduction	i–ii
CHAPTER 1 Theory and Practice	1
CHAPTER 2 Change and Development in the Later Empire	12
CHAPTER 3 The Army in Peace and War: Literary Evidence	23
CHAPTER 4 Later Documentary Evidence	33
CHAPTER 5 Archaeological Evidence	50
CHAPTER 6 Conclusions	59
Afterword	66
BIBLIOGRAPHY	67

INTRODUCTION

The Roman Army is one of the best documented institutions of the Ancient world but there are nevertheless areas of its structure and operations where the modern scholar is tantalisingly under-informed. The sizes of the various types of units composing the Army of the fourth and early fifth centuries A.D. is such an area. The issue of individual unit sizes is of course also of interest for the earlier Empire, but that period has at least produced a small body of explicit evidence in the form of various sorts of unit and sub-unit registers – few of which appear to have been extraordinarily small. Such direct evidence however does not appear to have survived for periods beyond the early years of the third century.

Until recent years rather more consideration has in fact been given to the <u>overall</u> size of the Imperial defence forces, with individual unit establishments having been treated as a side issue. Thus, Ramsay MacMullen in 1980[1] epitomised the estimates of some twenty scholars writing from 1914 onwards to present a range of army totals between a low of 200,000 and an absolute maximum of no fewer than 1,000,000 men. For the fourth and early fifth centuries, MacMullen cites calculations from 200,000 to 737,000.

In 1961 L. Várady[2] had attempted some quite detailed computations for both overall numbers and unit sizes in the army of the fifth century. He suggested quite a complicated series of unit establishments considerably reduced in size from the assumed norms of the Principate but in effect these amounted to little more than educated guesses. Although certain evidence had long existed in terms of, for instance, literary references to unit sizes, it is arguable that the breakthrough for this subject came with the publication in Dublin in 1964 of fragmentary papyri from the files of the <u>strategus</u> at Panopolis in Upper Egypt dating from AD 298-300. Although not explicitly providing information about unit sizes, these documents record details of the transfer of quantities of cash and supplies to various units of the Egyptian garrison. A.H.M. Jones in 1964[3] and Richard Duncan-Jones in 1978[4] extrapolated from the Panopolis papyri unit sizes for the Diocletianic army. These estimates, and especially the greatly reduced estimates of Duncan-Jones, have become central to the debate and widely accepted. A major element of this thesis will be a critique of these assessments and of the generalisations that have been based on them.

The other central element of the case for significantly reduced unit sizes is the evidence of archaeology and especially the apparently diminutive garrisons of certain British forts housed in newly contructed 'chalets' or family units. The chalet argument was first presented in detail by John Wilkes in 1966[5] and has since gained very wide currency. That argument will also be analysed.

Roger Tomlin is an eminent example of a proponent for the case that the Roman Army contained units of very small size by the early 4th century.[6] That case will be presented and examined in this thesis. The approach will be based essentially on a study of the primary written sources, both documentary and literary, and interpretations of these sources but some attention will also be paid to archaeological evidence.

The issue of unit sizes is of more than marginal interest and its implications have generally been somewhat neglected. Small units might, for instance, imply a different attitude towards fort defence and the need to withstand sieges. It might also support a case that units must have changed their internal structures, and would have found the outposting of sub-units – which increasingly appears to have been characteristic of the first century – more difficult. The scale of military engagements in the Late Empire might also have been of a different nature had army units been smaller. Smaller units do not of course necessarily mean a smaller army, but where fort or provincial garrisons were reduced there would have been economic consequences of at least a

---

[1] Ramsay MacMullen, 'How Big was the Roman Imperial Army?', **Klio**, Band 62 (1980), Berlin, pages 451-460.
[2] L. Várady, 'New Evidences on Some Problems of the Late Roman Military Organisation', **Acta Antiqua Academiae Scientiarium Hungaricae** Tomus 9, Budapest, 1961, pages 333-96.
[3] A.H.M. Jones, **The Later Roman Empire 284-602: A Social, Economic and Administrative Survey**, Oxford, 1964.
[4] R.P. Duncan-Jones, 'Pay and Numbers in Diocletian's Army', **Chiron**, Band 8 (1978), München, pages 541-60. A revised version was published as chapter 7 of Richard Duncan-Jones' **Structure and Scale in the Roman Economy**, Cambridge, 1990, pages 105-17.
[5] J.J. Wilkes, 'Early fourth century rebuilding in Hadrian's Wall forts' in M.G. Jarrett and B. Dobson [edd.], **Britain and Rome**, Kendal, 1966, pages 114-138.
[6] Roger Tomlin, 'The Late-Roman Empire' in General Sir John Hackett (ed.), **Warfare in the Ancient World**, London, 1989 and 'The Mobile Army' in Peter Connolly (ed.), **Greece and Rome at War**, London 1981, pages 249-259.

local nature. Most significant perhaps is a possible connection between units smaller as a result of decay rather than deliberate planning and the military setbacks of the fourth and fifth centuries. Was the decline of Rome and the fall of the Western Empire partly the consequence of invading forces being opposed by army units with declining troop numbers?

Such a re-examination of the evidence for unit sizes in the Late Empire should throw light on the sort of questions raised above. Many modern studies incorporate bold and sweeping assertions about unit sizes in the Later Roman Army and, based on such generalisations, proceed to further broad statements about the Late Army in general and even about Late Antiquity as a whole. This enquiry will also involve an evaluation of the interpretations of the evidence, and thus an examination of the validity of the generalisations most commonly put forward in secondary works.

CHAPTER 1

THEORY AND PRACTICE

Although the army of the Late Empire contained a number of new types of units and of units based on earlier types but much altered, it will be useful briefly to glance at those earlier formations and to attempt to establish some sort of base-lines from which to look at later developments.

The army of the Early Empire was a much simpler organisation than that of the Late Empire and contained a fairly limited number of types of units. Leaving aside elements of the Fleet and the Praetorian Guard (as well as what we might consider para-military units such as the vigiles and cohortes urbanae), the army of the Early Empire was composed of the Legions and the Auxiliaries.

The Legions

It is generally agreed that, from a peak of some sixty legions at the time of the Battle of Actium (31 BC), Augustus created an Imperial Army that included some 28. During the next two centuries or so, this figure remained remarkably constant: the low point was apparently the 25 legions reached following the Varian disaster in AD 9 (a figure not increased for some 30-33 years), with the total peaking at thirty legions in perhaps AD 68/70, c. AD 101 and c. AD 165.[1]

It is indicative of the problems involved in assessing Roman Army unit sizes that, as Keppie remarked, '. . . surprisingly the precise total [sc. of men in a legion] is nowhere reliably attested.'[2]

Writing during the reign of Augustus, Livy put the strength of a legion in 340 BC at 5,000 infantry and 300 cavalry.[3] The Greek historian Polybius, writing in the second century BC and referring to his own times, said that a legion included 300 cavalry and 4,200 infantry, which could be increased 'in times of exceptional danger' to a total of 5,000.[4]

This seems to provide a basis for estimating legionary strengths during the mid/late Republic of perhaps 4,500-5,300. This is not a greatly different range from estimates that can be produced for the Early Empire, and it is interesting to note that the Byzantine antiquarian, John Lydus, writing in the mid-sixth century AD but purporting to refer to 388 BC, gave legions a strength of 6,000 infantry.[5]

The Early Imperial legions were organised rather differently from Republican ones and our basis for calculating their size is the explicit statement in the anonymous treatise on laying out fortifications attributed to 'Hyginus': '... plena centuria habet milites LXXX.'[6] Excavation of fortress plans also makes it clear that, whatever may once or theoretically have been true, accommodation was invariably provided for eighty rather than a hundred men per centuria.

Six centuries of eighty men each would have made a cohort 480 strong and given a legion an establishment of 4,800 men but there is the additional complication that by the late first century AD the First Cohort had developed a structure quite different from the other nine: it had not six centuries but five and those of double strength (160 men). The First Cohort of a legion contained therefore not the standard 480 men but 800. This should have produced a legionary total of 5,120 men (9 x 480 = 4,320 + 800) but there needs also to be considered the fact that the legion also included, in addition to its infantry, a small force of 120 mounted troops - used apparently as scouts and messengers. It seems most probable that these troopers were carried on the books of the cohorts rather than additionally and that therefore the actual establishment of a legion was 5,120. If this view is mistaken and the mounted element was supernumerary, then the legionary establishment would have been 5,240 men.

---

[1] Cf. J.C. Mann, **Legionary Recruitment and Veteran Settlement during the Principate**, Insitute of Archaeology Occasional Publications No. 7, London, 1983.
[2] Lawrence Keppie, **The Making of the Roman Army: From Republic to Empire**, London, 1984, page 173.
[3] Livy, **Ab urbe condita**, 8, 8.
[4] Polybius, **Histories**, 6, 20.
[5] John Lydus, **On Powers**, 1, 46.
[6] 'Hyginus', **de metatione castrorum**, 1. Dates from the late first century to the fourth century have been suggested for the composition of this work.

These considerations allow for no final certainty but it will be a reasonably safe generalisation to state that by the late first century AD a legion's theoretical strength was just in excess of 5,000.

The Auxiliaries

The need for non-legionary forces raised outside the citizen body and performing functions not well served by the legions – such as cavalry and light infantry – had arisen intermittently under the Republic, and such forces had been raised on an ad hoc basis. Even by the beginning of the Empire many of these auxiliary units may not have had a permanent existence but have been disbanded when no longer needed. Very large numbers of such formations were however gathered during the Civil Wars and the reign of Augustus: the Balkan expeditionary force of AD 7, for example, included not only ten legions but no fewer than 86 auxiliary units.[7]

By the Early Empire, and possibly under Augustus, auxiliary units became regular elements of the Army and acquired their standardised organisations and sizes. The majority of auxiliary formations were nominally 500 strong but a large minority were theoretically double this size. During the second half of the first century AD 'mixed' units – of both infantry and cavalry – emerged, and by then six different types of units can be distinguished:

1. The most common type was the quingenary peditate cohort, an infantry 'battalion' of 500 men. 'Hyginus' stated[8] that these comprised six centuries. Although the reference in 'Hyginus'[9] to the strength of centuries is legionary and there is no explicit evidence on this point elsewhere, it seems reasonable to assign these centuries also strengths of eighty men each, giving these units total establishments of 480 which obviously matches quite closely with the nominal quingenary size. One calculation is that there were 127 such units in existence by c. AD 150.[10]

2. Milliary peditate cohorts were double-sized infantry units developed under the Early Empire: one of the first records of such a unit dates from AD 88.[11] According to 'Hyginus', they consisted not of 12 centuries (as might have been expected) but of ten:[12] legionary-sized centuries would have put these units at 800 men. It has been suggested alternatively that, in this case, centuries of 100 men should be assumed bringing the cohorts to their nominal milliary strength. There are however obvious difficulties in arguing that the Roman Army operated centuries of different sizes. It has been calculated that there were no more than perhaps 18 of these large formations in the mid-first century.[13]

3. The most common cavalry units were quingenary alae. There are two ancient references for calculating their size: 'Hyginus' wrote that they comprised 16 turmae (or 'squadrons')[14] and Arrian that they totalled 512 men.[15] The turma size which these two figures produce (32) coincides neatly with the figure Vegetius gave for a legionary cavalry turma.[16] The squadron commanders, the decurions, seem not to have been included in Arrian's figures: their inclusion would take the unit size to 528 (512 + 16). It remains unclear however whether the two junior officers in each turma, the duplicarius and the sesquiplicarius, should or should not be included in the totals and therefore whether there were thirty or 32 actual troopers. The mid-second century total of quingenary alae has been calculated at some 82-90 units (with perhaps up to about 15 stationed in Britain).[17]

4. The rare milliary alae consisted of 24 turmae, according to 'Hyginus', although 32

---

[7] Cf. Velleius (Paterculus), **Historia Romana**, 2, 113, 1 and Keppie, ibid., page 166.
[8] 'Hyginus', 28.
[9] Ibid., 1.
[10] By Dr Brian Dobson, 'The Empire' in **Warfare in the Ancient World**, edited by General Sir John Hackett, London, 1989, pages 192-221.
[11] **CIL** 16, 35 (7 November 88).
[12] 'Hyginus', 28.
[13] Cf. Dobson, op. cit.
[14] 'Hyginus', 16.
[15] Arrian, **Tactica**, 18.
[16] Vegetius, **Epitoma rei militaris**, 2, 14. A turma total of 32 might be seen as representing four 'standard' contubernia of eight men each. Record no. 80 (= P. Lond. 482) in Robert O. Fink. **Roman Military Records on Papyrus** (Philological Monographs of the American Philological Association No. 26, Cleveland, Ohio, 1971), which is a hay receipt dating from May (?) AD 130 for a turma of the ala veterana Gallica, on the other hand, lists thirty names: a total of 31 if the decurion is added. Ch LA XI n501 (a fragment of a pridianum of ala Commagenorum from the Claudian period) records 434 men and 12 decurions, which might be taken as showing 36 men per turma (434 ÷ 12 = 36.166) but it is not clear if all the decurions were present: if there were actually 16 turmae (with four decurions absent), then the turma size average would fall to about 27.
[17] Cf. Dobson, op. cit. (note 10) and P. A. Holder, **The Roman Army in Britain**, London, 1982, pages 107-112.

might have been anticipated.[18] 24 turmae of 32 men each produce a unit size of 768, which some feel falls rather short of the nominal thousand. It has been argued by von Domaszewski[19] on the basis of an inscription from Coptos that the turmae of milliary alae were not 32 but 42 strong: this would put the establishment of such a unit at 1,008. It is far from clear however that the Coptos inscription does in fact record, as von Domaszewski claimed, a vexillation from three alae with 424 troopers under ten officers: it can also be interpreted as referring to five squadron commanders (the five <u>decuriones</u>) and their five subordinate officers. This would then have no relevance to establishing the turma size in these units.

Breeze and Dobson have argued[20] that these milliary alae should be seen not so much as 'double' sized units but rather as 'one-and-a-halfers', which a strength of 768 would make them.[21] Inclusion of 24 decurions would produce a grand total of 792.

Another way of producing a total closer to the nominal 1,000 would be to allow each of 24 turmae not 32 men but forty: forty men could represent five contuberniae. There is no evidential basis for assuming forty-strong turmae but this suggestion would give an ala of 960 men.

In any case it is these rare units, rather than the legions, which should perhaps be seen as the élite shock troops of the Early Empire: a strike force of at least 750 horsemen would hardly fail to impress. They would be expensive to maintain and this might help to explain why the normal total for these units across the Empire was no more than between eight and ten: only one was stationed in Britain.[22]

5. Real problems arise when we begin to look at possible sizes for the part-mounted equitate cohorts, units which R.W. Davies has described as one of the few major military innovations of the Principate.[23] An inscription from late in the reign of Augustus[24] is perhaps the earliest record of such a unit, or at least a prototype. Quingenary equitate cohorts had six centuries and 120 cavalry, according to 'Hyginus',[25] but of course 120 does not divide by 32. We might however assume four turmae of only thirty each (4 x 30 = 120) or argue that the 120 of 'Hyginus' was an approximation for 128, which would allow turmae of 32 (4 x 32 = 128). Alternatively, it has been suggested that quingenary equitate cohorts might have included five rather than four turmae: five turmae each of three standard eight-strong contubernia and five turmae each of four smaller contubernia of only six men each both produce exactly 120 troopers. Although most documentary evidence points to four turmae as a norm, the well documented Twentieth Palmyrenes from Dura had five and fort plans can be found to support both possibilities.

What infantry strength are we then to allow such a cohort? The norm for centuries of eighty men, as in the case of legions and quite probably auxiliary cohorts too, would give an equitate cohort an infantry component of 480 (6 x 80 = 480). We could then calculate a unit size of 600 or 608 (480 + 120 or 480 + 128), which seems a reasonable approximation for the nominal size of 500. If it is felt however, as some have argued, that the important consideration in making these calculations is to produce a unit as close as possible to the the nominal size, then centuries of 72 (nine contubernia of eight each), 64 (eight contubernia of eight each) or sixty (ten smaller contubernia of only six each) have all been proposed as possibilities.

Table 2 lists some of the complicated permutations which result from these alternative suggestions: as well as the 600 or 608 already considered, unit sizes of 480, 488, 504, 512, 552 and 560 also then become possibilities. The Empire in the mid-second century contained some 130 equitate cohorts: the bulk

---

[18] 'Hyginus', 16.
[19] A. von Domaszewski, **Die Rangordnung des römisches Heeres**, Cologne, 1967, page 35. The inscription is **CIL** 3, 6627. Eric Birley, 'Alae and Cohortes Milliariae' in **Corolla memoriae Erich Swoboda Dedicata**, Römische Forschungen in Niederösterreich V, 1966, pages 54-67 [reprinted in Mavors IV pages 349-364) also argues for 42-strong turmae in milliary units (and incidentally for three different century sizes – of 100, eighty and sixty).
[20] David J. Breeze and Brian Dobson, **Hadrian's Wall**, London, 1976, pages 154-6.
[21] Is it not also possible however that a copying error could have transformed XXXII in 'Hyginus' into XXIIII?
[22] See Dobson, op. cit. (note 10), page 198 and E. Birley, op. cit. (note 19), pages 351-2. The example from Britain was the ala Augusta Gallorum Petriana milliaria CR bis torquata based at Stanwix from probably the early second century until it was attested there by the Notitia: cf. Holder, op. cit. (note 17) pages 108-9.

[23] R.W. Davies, 'Cohortes Equitate' in **Historia**, Band 20, Wiesbaden, 1971, pages 751-63.
[24] **CIL** 10, 4862 (= **ILS** 2690), which attests cohors Ubiorum peditum et equitum.
[25] 'Hyginus', 27.

of the cohorts in Britain (perhaps 25 or slightly more) were of this type.[26]

6. Finally, there were the milliary equitate cohorts: part-mounted units nominally 1,000-strong. Although 'Hyginus' stated a precise structure for these regiments (ten centuries with 760 infantry and ten turmae of 240 cavalry),[27] a wide range of alternatives have nevertheless been proposed. The figures given by 'Hyginus' would produce centuries of 76 men but the legionary norm of eighty would raise the infantry component to 800 men. This could be further varied to 600, 640 or 720 to accommodate century sizes of sixty, 64 or 72 men respectively. If the cavalry figure given by 'Hyginus' is accepted, there would already then be unit size possibilities of 840, 880, 960, 1,000 and 1,040.

Further complications are produced by the suggestions that turma numbers must have been eight rather than ten and that turma sizes must have been thirty or 32 rather than 24. The basis for assuming eight turmae is that the text of 'Hyginus' is corrupt at this point and that eight would neatly double the four that may have applied to quingenary equitate cohorts. Thirty or 32 troopers have already been argued, and it is worth noting that eight turmae of thirty men each exactly matches the 240 troopers of 'Hyginus', while eight turmae of 32 each comes close at 256.

Table 2 lays out the complex permutations produced by the various suggestions for these units: there are 21 possible structures and 16 possible sizes. The total number of such units in the Empire in the mid-second century was perhaps no higher than about 22.[28]

It is very difficult to conclude then that our base-lines for unit size assumptions for the situation by the end of the first century are very solidly drawn, although some seem firmer than others and in any case the range of possibilities suggested for any particular unit type is not ridiculously wide: at the largest [milliary equitate cohorts] the top end of the scale is no more than 36% higher than the bottom. Even with these official, theoretical establishments however, it is perhaps necessary to consider that - in some cases at least - our primary literary sources are mistaken or corrupt or partly so. Secondly, terminology (especially distributive numbers) is not being employed with any great precision. Thirdly, the Roman Army may have used the same unit or sub-unit term to describe formations of quite different sizes.

Documentary Evidence

Theory is of course one thing: practice, all too frequently, quite another. Many examples of modern institutions - military or otherwise - could be cited where official structures or sizes have little to do with reality. A small number of Roman Army documents survive from the first to the early third centuries, against which we can attempt to collate the unit sizes suggested above.

1. Chronologically, the first document to be considered is the recently discovered strength report from Vindolanda of cohors I Tungrorum.[29] This is the only major document yet found from the earliest [1.42-hectare/3.5-acre] fort on the site (occupied c. AD 85/90): it probably dates however from slightly later, 18th May of a year unknown but probably AD 92-7 and is possibly an interim monthly return. It puts the net strength (numerus purus) of the unit at 752 men including six centurions. A striking proportion of the unit was absent from base: 46 were serving as guards of the governor 'at the office of Ferox';[30] no fewer than 337 (45% of the cohort's strength) including two centurions were at 'Coria' (probably Corbridge); a centurion was in London; and 72 other soldiers, including two centurions, were distributed among five posts which cannot be identified. In other words 456 men (61% of the total) including five out of six centurions were away from base. Of the remaining 296, 31 were ill (including six from wounds and apparently ten with eye problems) leaving only 265 men with just a

---

[26] Dobson, loc. cit. (note 10), and Holder, op. cit. (note 17) pages 112-124.
[27] 'Hyginus', 26 and 27. 'Hyginus' actually wrote (27): 'Habet itaque cohors equitata milliaria centurias X peditum, equites CCXL turmas decuriones.' A numeral has evidently dropped out after 'turmas' and it is usually assumed that the original text read not 'turmas decuriones' but 'turmas decem' or 'turmas X'.
[28] Dobson, loc. cit. (note 10).

[29] Alan K. Bowman and J. David Thomas,' A Military Strength Report From Vindolanda' in **JRS** 81, London, 1991, pages 15-26. See also Robin Birley, 'Vindolanda' in **Current Archaeology** 116, London, August 1989, pages 275-9, 'Vindolanda' in **Current Archaeology** 128, London, March 1992, pages 344-9, A. R. Birley, 'Vindolanda: new writing tablets 1986-89' in V. A. Maxfield & M.J. Dobson [edd.], **Roman Frontier Studies** 1989, Exeter, 1992, pages 6 ff., and Alan K. Bowman, **Life and Letters on the Roman Frontier**, London, 1994, 1, pages 104-5.
[30] Bowman & Thomas, op. cit. (note 29) [=Vindolanda Inv. no. 88/841], lines 5/6: 'singulares leg(ati) xlvi officio ferocis'. Bowman (1994) suggests that Ferox may have been the legate of IX Hispana at York.

single centurion (35%) present at the cohort's base and fit for action.

The editors assume[31] that the cohort was of the milliary peditate type. It is known from other evidence that the unit was milliary by AD 103, reduced to quingenary by AD 122 but milliary again by AD 146.[32] If milliary, the unit was evidently under-strength (although a respectable 94% of a nominal 800) and included only six centurions. As well as the outside possibility that the unit was actually an over-strength quingenary one, it has also been suggested that it may have been a cohort in the process of re-organising from quingenary to milliary strength.[33] If the tablet is correctly assigned to the earliest Vindolanda fort, then there is the further oddity that that site could never have held the whole strength recorded in the document, although it could have accommodated more than the 250-odd it actually did. There may of course have been other units at Vindolanda at this time but we must also note the strong possibility that Roman Army forts were - at least at this period - not intended ever to house the whole of their garrison units.[34] There is an important implication here for the lessons that can be drawn from archaeological evidence.

2. Another early document is the one known as 'Hunt's **pridianum**', an annual return for cohors I Hispanorum veterana stationed at Stobi in Macedonia probably in the period AD 105/108.[35] The papyrus puts the unit's strength at 546, including 119 cavalry, under six centurions and four decurions. This is evidently a quingenary equitate cohort with probably four slightly under-strength 32-strong turmae or perhaps four turmae very close to an establishment of thirty.[36] Mark Hassall has suggested alternatively that one decurion was absent and that there were in fact five turmae each with a theoretical establishment of 24 and therefore at 99.2% of strength.[37]

The infantry element of the cohort can be assumed by a process of deduction (546 - 119) to have totalled 427 men. Divided by six, this produces a century average of just over 71.[38] As it is difficult to argue for the cohort having had turmae under-strength but centuries not, the simplest interpretation is to accept the obvious: that the cohort had six centuries each at average strength of about 90%[39] of an establishment of eighty.

This pridianum demonstrates incidentally the Roman Army's predilection for detaching small forces from a parent unit. Apart from small numbers (or perhaps individual soldiers) detached, the cohort had a garrison based at Piroboridava in the Sereth (Hierasus) Valley over 650 kilometres [400 miles] from HQ; a scouting patrol across the Danube; and an expedition with 23 troopers, at least one decurion, and a centurion (with presumably some infantry too) also across the Danube. Although only the last element can be even provisionally quantified, the cohort had a substantial minority of its troops away from its base - in some cases, surprising distances away.

3. A pridianum of the cohors I Augusta Praetoria Lusitanorum equitata has been found dating from 31 August 156.[40] Total strength is put at 505, including six centurions with 363 infantry (an average of 60.5 men per century). A nominal century establishment of eighty would make these centuries rather weak

---

[31] Ibid., page 19.
[32] Ibid., loc. cit., quoting **CIL** 16, 48, **CIL** 16, 69–70 and **RIB** 2155.
[33] Cf. 'Vindolanda', op. cit. (note 29) [1992], page 347 quoting Eric Birley.
[34] Cf. J.C. Mann, 'The historical development of the Saxon Shore' in Valerie A. Maxfield [ed.], **The Saxon Shore: A Handbook**, Exeter Studies in History No. 25, Exeter, 1989, page 1: '... the normal situation for any unit, in any period of history, is that it is fragmented, and distributed in several different places.... If a unit in any offical list is assigned to any particular place, in all probability that place will merely be the location of unit HQ, nothing more. Some elements are quite likely to be elsewhere.'
[35] See British Museum Papyrus 2851, published as No. 63 in Robert O. Fink, op. cit. (note 16); Robert O. Fink, 'Hunt's Pridianum: British Museum Papyrus 2851' in **JRS** 48, London, 1958 pages 102–116; Ronald Syme, 'The Lower Danube under Trajan' in **JRS** 49, London, pages 26–33; J.F. Gilliam, 'The Moesian 'Pridianum' in **Homages à Albert Grenier**, Brussels, 1962, pages 747–756; and Mark Hassall, 'The Internal Planning of Roman Auxiliary Forts' in Brian Hartley and John Wacher, **Rome and Her Northern Provinces**, Gloucester, 1983, pages 96–131. Fink argued originally for a date of AD 99, and later for c. 17 September 100, 101, 104 or 105; Syme's preference for AD 105/108 is now however widely accepted. Although stationed at Stobi in Macedonia, the cohort formed part of the army of Moesia Inferior.
[36] 119 ÷ 4 = 29.75. Gilliam, op. cit. (note 35), page 748 argued for a total strength (with accessions) of 596.
[37] 119 ÷ 5 = 23.8.
[38] 71.166.
[39] 88.9575%.
[40] Published as No. 64 in Fink, **RMR** = Berlin Papyrus No. 696 col. 1 = **Select Papyri** No. 401 = **American Journal of Philology** 63 (1942), pages 61–71 and 73 (1952), pages 75–8. Translation published as No. 153 in Naphtali Lewis and Meyer Reinhold [edd.], **Roman Civilization Sourcebook II: The Empire**, New York, 1955, page 517. See also Hassall, op. cit. (note 35). Note that the Egyptian calendar ended in August.

(75.65% of maximum) but this would not be unreasonable in conditions of relative peace: the unit had been at the same station opposite Apollonopolis Maior in the Thebaid for 25 years. It might otherwise be calculated that the centuries of this cohort were at full strength meant to comprise not eighty but either sixty or 64 men each, in which case they would actually have averaged in AD 156 100.8% or 94.5% of establishment.

The pridianum gives the cohort 114 troopers but only three decurions. Assuming that there were in fact four turmae, this would mean each contained an average 28.5 men, which might represent 89% of a nominal 32. This is a plausible calculation but it might otherwise be suggested that the turmae were at full strength thirty strong and therefore in this case at 95% of establishment, or perhaps that there were in fact five 24-strong turmae in this cohort each actually averaging 22.8 men (or again 95% of nominal strength). As usual however the simplest assumption remains the most attractive.

It can be noted that this unit appears in the Notitia Dignitatum still stationed in Egypt, although 155 kilometres [250 miles] down the Nile at Hieracon (Der el Gebrawi).[41] Although the disposition of the forces under the dux Thebaidos recorded in the Notitia are apparently Diocletianic, it nevertheless implies that the cohors I Lusitanorum had been based in Egypt for well over a century and a half, and perhaps even longer.

4. First published in 1977 is the pridianum of an unidentified quingenary equitate cohort stationed in Egypt, possibly in the Thebaid. The editors suggest that the unit is identical to the one in the previous example – cohors I Lusitanorum – but this identification is far from certain.[42]

The pridianum dates from 213/216, and probably from 215.[43] The cohort it records contained four decurions with 100 troopers plus 13 camel-riders. Total strength is given as 457 and the six centurions recorded presumably therefore commanded 334 infantrymen – an average of 55.7 men each.[44] Assuming four decurions represent four turmae, each turma would have contained 25 troopers on average.[45]

The papyrus does apparently record permanent losses of thirty men ('decesserunt') from the cohort, including an unknown number posted to the Fleet,[46] seven killed (in action?) and one invalided out. These permanent losses imply an original unit strength of 487. Only about three-quarters of the cohort was actually present at its base: the pridianum records 126 men (just over 27% of total) 'absunt in choram'.[47] These soldiers posted to the countryside may have been, the editors suggest, stationed in the Delta to help deal with the disturbances following Caracalla's visit in 215.

5. The only substantial files of a Roman Army unit ever to have been discovered are those of cohors XX Palmyrenorum from Dura-Europos in Syria Coele. Originally a Seleucid fortress built in 300 BC, the city of Dura had been briefly under Roman control during the reign of Trajan (AD 115-117) and was recaptured by Lucius Verus during his Parthian expedition of AD 165 and thereafter retained until its destruction by Persian forces under Shapur I in 256. Dura was in an important position, lying at the centre of the district along the Euphrates known as the Parapotamia and also directly on the principal route from lower Mesopotamia into northern Syria; the whole Euphrates line formed a major element of the frontier between Rome and its Iranian neighbours (the Parthians and later the Sassanids), and Dura was one of a string of strong outposts along it.

For the first thirty or forty years of the main Roman occupation very little is known about Dura. It seems to have had a small garrison, at least partly composed of Palmyrene archers – as had been the case during the late Parthian period. The unit that is of particular concern here, the cohors XX Palmyrenorum, is first attested at Dura on 16th March AD 208 (P. Dura 56) but may well have been in existence considerably longer – possibly from the 190s or even 170s.[48] The cohort is known only from

---

[41] **Notitia Dignitatum** Or. 31, 58. The cohort's station in this document, 'contra Apollonopolis', was itself occupied according to the **Notitia** by a cavalry regiment, ala I Francorum.
[42] J.D. Thomas and R.W. Davies, 'A New Military Strength Report on Papyrus' in **JRS** 67, London, 1977, pages 50-61.
[43] Ibid., page 57.
[44] Alternative average century strengths are 92.8% of 60, 87% of 64, 77.4% of 72 and 69.9% of 80.
[45] This would be 78% of 32, 83.3% of 30 or 104.2% of 24.
[46] As a disciplinary measure, the editors suggest.
[47] Thomas and Davies, op. cit. (note 42), Col. II, line 13.
[48] C.B. Welles, R.O. Fink and J.F.Gilliam, **The Excavations at Dura-Europos: Final Report V, Part 1. The Parchments and Papyri**, New Haven, 1959. See

the papyri from its own archive and from inscriptions from the city. It was presumably lost or formally disbanded when the Persians captured Dura.

The records of the cohort are an extremely rich source but, for the present purpose, they arguably create more problems than they solve. The archive includes two extremely rare complete working rosters (of the type called 'Morning Reports' by Fink): they are probably about three or four years apart in date. The earlier roster was dated by its editors to AD 219[49] and lists all the men of the unit grouped by centuries and turmae. Strangely enough there are six of the former and five of the latter, which of course corresponds to none of the equitate cohort structures already suggested, either quingenary or milliary. The century sizes vary considerably from a minimum of about 69 to well over 140: all but one century have strengths in three figures.[50] It can be seen therefore that, on one of the rare occasions when reality is recorded in detail, it bears only a slight resemblance to theory. Average century size for XX Palmyrenorum in 219 works out in the range 121/123 – i.e. over 50% larger than the usual assumed norm of eighty. One complication to be borne is mind is that actual totals survive only for three of the cohort's centuries and these in only one case match tidily with what a damaged papyrus seems to record in terms of names. Thus, for example, the century of Marcus is given as containing a total of 140 soldiers but the papyrus only includes some 105 actual names with lacunae implying another 24 or so – for a total of about 129.[51] Similarly, the papyrus's editors put the total of names for the century of Aurelius Julius Marianus at 114 with about 25 names lost for a total of some 139 men (compared with the recorded total of 146).[52] What might therefore have appeared to be a fairly standard quingenary equitate cohort in fact had five of its six centuries greatly over-strength, in some cases nearly double the probable norm of eighty men each.

The turmae of XX Palmyrenorum are equally far removed in practice from the theories discussed above – to a positively bizarre degree. Bearing in mind the usual turma size assumption of 32, the Dura cohort in contrast contained turmae with claimed total sizes of 140/149, 130/139, 122/131, 120/139 and 134. In other words, theory would have given these five turmae no more than 160 men while the roster actually records squadron totals giving the cohort no fewer than 646 cavalry and perhaps as many as 692 – four times more than might have been expected! On the other hand, as with the infantry element of the unit, the roster details do not support the claimed squadron totals given above. They are respectively 60, 66, 68, 71 and 61/67 men: although much lower than the claimed totals, these figures are of course very large – in the region of double the assumed norm of 32 – and still push the cavalry element of the unit well beyond the theoretical maximum of 160 to something in the region of 326/332. With the first four turmae incidentally, the papyrus has no lacunae and the totals provided by the names listed can be taken as indisputably accurate totals.

We are left then, on the evidence of P. Dura 100, with a very strange unit both in terms of structure and size. It also appears to be a unit with a theoretical or paper strength considerably higher than its actual numbers. Counting the names that can actually be read a total of 945 is reached; this is surely an incontrovertible minimum but gaps in the papyrus can be assumed to push this up to some 1,054. An additional 16 dromedarii then create a grand total of 1,070 men. The unit sub-total figures however claim an enormous strength for the cohort of something between 1,390 and 1,451 men. It may be that what is recorded here is a normal quingenary equitate cohort heavily reinforced because of the critical situation on

---

also Fink, **RMR** and Michael H. Dodgeon and Samuel N.C. Lieu [edd.], **The Roman Eastern Frontier and the Persian Wars AD 226-363: A documentary History**, London & New York, 1991.

[49] P. Dura 100. The dating is based on the enlistment dates in the documents. It does however create the possible anomaly that the century of Malchius, although designated '> Malchi' in P. Dura 101, appears as '> Malchiana' in P. Dura 100, the supposedly earlier document. This adjectical form of the name was normally used for a *centuria* awaiting a new centurion when its previous commander had died, retired or been transferred. It could be that the editors have reversed the dates of these two papyri, or that two centurions of similar names are concerned.

[50] The roster lists for the century of Danymus include some 55 names and there are gaps implying another 14 or so (= c. 69+); for the century of Marcus about 105 names or fragmentary names and gaps implying about 24 or more (= c. 129/141 allowing for 12 lines lost); for the century of Aurelius Dometius Antoninus about 110 names and gaps allowing for another 15 or so (= c. 125+); for the century of Aurelius Castricius about 96 names and perhaps 12 lost (= c. 108+); for the century of Aurelius Julius Marianus 114 names and c. 25 lost (= c. 139); and for the centuria Malchiana 139 names and c. five lost (= c. 144).

[51] P. Dura 100, cols. 6-10.
[52] P. Dura 100, cols. 21-26, 12.

the Eastern frontier (it was after all only 37 years after this document was compiled that Dura was lost to the Persians), or that it was a milliary unit from which a vexillation (of four out of ten centuries and three out of eight turmae) had been permanently detached and then this reduced structure was doubled to serve as a guard 'unit' for a Governor or Dux. There remains the problem however of the gross inflation of the paper strength of the turmae: the cohort was apparently carrying some 316–362 'ghost' troopers. This practice is certainly known from other periods of history and may well have been a semi–official custom to allow for the drawing of extra rations and/or pay. Why however should the unit only create 'ghost' cavalrymen? The answer might relate to the fact that the cavalry was better paid than the infantry but it is still hard not to wonder if the Imperial Treasury would not have been likely to notice fraud on quite such a scale.

The Dura archive also included a series of 'morning reports' dating from a March in an unknown year between AD 223 and 235 (possibly 233). On 27 March, for instance, the cohort totalled 923[53] including 223 cavalry; there were nine centurions (although only six centuries), five decurions, twenty junior officers and 34 camel–riders. The figures for the next two days are not complete (92– and 9––) but on 30 March the cohort strength was down to 914 men. The fluid nature of unit establishments is illustrated by this 1% loss of strength in four days.

Further Dura records give strengths of 781 at its base ('in hibernis'), including perhaps 185 (or 233) cavalry, on 27 and 28 May 239;[54] 766 milites and 226 (?) absentees at a date in c. 225/235;[55] and apparently 389 equites at a date unknown.[56] All things considered, the Dura materials present a very odd and confusing picture.

6. Robert Marichal published in 1979 an article on the discovery at Bu Njem in Libya of some 146 ostraca, of which 117 relate to matters military.[57] Although Bu Njem's garrison between AD 201 and 238 included a vexillation of legio III Augusta, the nine ostraca that are dated are from the 250s and apparently refer to a numerus based in the fort under a decurion. Although Marichal printed only one ostracon in full, the others apparently included a number of century daily reports. The number of effectives varied from 42 to 63 men, averaging 57. These are fairly weak sub–unit strengths if we assume nominal century sizes of 80 (71% on average) but not unreasonably low.

Conclusions

Table 1 has been constructed to show the possible tables of organisation for quingenary equitate cohorts, the units for which the largest number of primary sources survive (although it needs to be stressed that these nevertheless represent a tiny and random sample). What does seem to emerge is that the two basic points of evidence provided by 'Hyginus' are well supported and therefore credible: namely, the units contained six centuries and 120 cavalrymen.

Cohors XX Palmyrenorum has been excluded from the list and, with this exception, it would be hard to argue for any other conclusion than that six centuries were standard, although the documentary evidence remains implicit rather than explicit. The cavalry component, as recorded by the documents, is strikingly homogenous: they come within 99.1%, 95% and 83.3% of the 'Hyginus' norm: it would be perverse not to acccept this norm as reality.

The infantry element however shows much more variety and this needs explanation. It may simply reflect the practicality that a smaller element is easier to keep up to strength than a larger one, or it may be more to do with the greater significance of the cavalry: they might have been regarded as the equivalent of a modern rapid reaction force. A number of suggestions have already been considered for the possible sizes of the infantry component of a

---

[53] Readings of 963 and 914 have also been suggested.
[54] P. Dura 89 = Fink, **RMR** No. 50. See also Dodgeon and Lieu, op. cit. (note 48), page 331. The apparently low numbers of the cohort at this point may reflect the situation following a battle against the Persians in which the unit's tribune, Julius Terentius, had been killed (**A.E.** 1948, 124). On the other hand, the phrase 'in hibernis' does imply the recording only of that element of the cohort not on detachment.
[55] P. Dura 91 = Fink, **RMR** No. 61. Does this mean a unit total of 992 or had the absentees already been discounted? Or does 766 'milites' specifically refer only to the cohort's infantry?
[56] P. Dura 92 = Fink, **RMR** No. 62. In addition P. Dura 83 (= Fink, **RMR** No. 48), dating from about 4 September 233, mentions 120 cavalry with XX Palmyrenorum; P. Dura 49 (= Fink, **RMR** No. 49), dating from possibly 218/222 or 238/244, mentions 140 cavalry and 32 camel–riders; P. Dura 92 (= Fink, **RMR** No. 62) apparently records 389 equites; and P. Dura 98

(= Fink, **RMR** No. 6) from AD 218/19 gives century strengths ranging from 52 to 58 (which would put the cohort's infantry total in the range of a maximum of 350).
[57] Robert Marichal, 'Les Ostraca de Bu Njem' in **Comptes Rendus de l'Academie des Inscriptions & Belles-Lettres**, 1979, pages 436–452.

quingenary equitate cohort: 360, 384, 432 or 480. There is no real room for ultimate certainty here but the general difficulty armies of any period have had in keeping forces above establishment might tend to create a preference for a figure larger than the largest actually recorded – that is, above 427. The fact that the existence of legionary centuries of eighty men is well attested might further incline us towards the calculation based on this assumption: that is, 480 infantrymen (six centuries of eighty each).

Although it must again be stressed that these figures (120 cavalry and 480 infantry = 600 men in a quingenary equitate cohort) can be claimed as no more than one strong possibility, it is interesting to note that on this basis the largest of the recorded such units would have had an impressive 99% of its troopers and a healthy 89% of its infantry.

It is always useful however to try to place our evidence in some sort of probability context and, if for the period covered by the examples in Table 1 (from the first decade of the second century to the second decade of the third), we accept Dobson's estimate of 130 such units and if we allow for no more than one strength report per annum (an unlikely minimum), then the three records we have represent survival of an absolute maximum of 0.02% of the originals. This is clearly very much random survival and should make us wary of concluding that any particular document demonstrates the typical.

Table 2 has been devised to show the literary evidence for unit structures and sizes together with the various interpretations of this evidence. It can be seen that the literary evidence is far from conclusive and remains open to a bewildering variety of interpretations, especially with the more complex unit types.

The documentary evidence, in conclusion, represents extremely limited random survival and the records of cohors XX Palmyrenorum, for example, create more problems than they solve. Until more evidence is discovered, we remain confined to probabilities, although in some cases the range of options is at least fairly limited.

Table 1: Possible Structure & Size models for Quingenary Equitate Cohorts (Literary & Documentary Evidence)

Source/Unit (Date)	Centuries	Infantry	Turmae	Cavalry	Size
'Hyginus' (2nd Century)	6			120	
Coh I Hisp vet (AD 105/108)	6 (prob.)	427	4 (prob.)	119	546/596(?)
Coh I Lusitanorum (AD 156)	6 (prob.)	363	4 (?)	114	505
? Coh (c. AD 215)	6 (prob.)	334	4 (prob.)	100	457/487

Table 2: Possible Establishments for Auxiliary Units

	Centuries	Infantry	Turmae	Cavalry	Size
A:	**Quingenary Peditate Cohort**				
'Hyginus'	6				
	6 x 80	480			480
B:	**Milliary Peditate Cohort**				
'Hyginus'	10				800
	10 x 80	800			800
	10 x 100	1,000			1,000
C:	**Quingenary Ala**				
'Hyginus'			16		
Arrian				512	512
Vegetius			-- x 32?		
			16 x 32	512	512/528
D:	**Milliary Ala**				

	Centuries	Infantry	Turmae	Cavalry	Size
'Hyginus'			24		
			24 x 32	768	768/792
			24 x 42	1,008	1,008
			24 x 40	960	960
E:	**Quingenary Equitate Cohort**				
'Hyginus'	6		120		
	6 x 60	360	4 x 30	120	480
	6 x 64	384	4 x 30	120	504
	6 x 72	432	4 x 30	120	552
	6 x 80	480	4 x 30	120	600
	6 x 60	360	4 x 32	128	488
	6 x 64	384	4 x 32	128	512
	6 x 72	432	4 x 32	128	560
	6 x 80	480	4 x 32	128	608
	6 x 60	360	5 x 24	120	480
	6 x 64	384	5 x 24	120	504
	6 x 72	432	5 x 24	120	552
	6 x 80	480	5 x 24	120	600

F: Milliary Equitate Cohort

'Hyginus'	10 x 76	760	10 x 24	240	1,000
	10 x 60	600	10 x 24	240	840
	10 x 64	640	10 x 24	240	880
	10 x 72	720	10 x 24	240	960
	10 x 80	800	10 x 24	240	1,040
	10 x 60	600	8 x 32	256	856
	10 x 64	640	8 x 32	256	896
	10 x 72	720	8 x 32	256	976
	10 x 80	800	8 x 32	256	1,056
	10 x 60	600	10 x 32	320	820
	10 x 64	640	10 x 32	320	860
	10 x 72	720	10 x 32	320	1,040
	10 x 80	800	10 x 32	320	1,120
	10 x 60	600	8 x 30	240	840
	10 x 64	640	8 x 30	240	880
	10 x 72	720	8 x 30	240	960
	10 x 80	800	8 x 30	240	1,040
	10 x 60	600	10 x 30	300	900
	10 x 64	640	10 x 30	300	940
	10 x 72	720	10 x 30	300	1,020
	10 x 80	800	10 x 30	300	1,100

CHAPTER 2

CHANGE AND DEVELOPMENT IN THE LATER EMPIRE

The structure of the army in the Early Empire was then, as we have seen, relatively simple. Excluding naval formations, the Praetorians, para-military forces and the numeri [a vague term meaning something like 'units'], we can describe the bulk of the army as comprising the legions and the auxiliaries – the latter being made up of six different types.

There seem to have been some 28 legions by the mid-second century, rising to 33 by the beginning of the next. Allowing each legion the establishment of 5,000 which we have seen as being the best estimate, there would therefore have been some 140,000 legionaries in c. AD 150 and perhaps 165,000 in c. AD 200. Estimating a total of auxiliary units is less straightforward but a variety of attempts have been made. Brian Dobson, for example, has calculated some 387 cohorts and alae by c. AD 150.[1] Eric Birley put the total for the same period at 409-419,[2] while Ramsay MacMullen would bring the total down half a century or so later to approximately 350.[3] Dobson uses his own estimates to put the total of auxiliaries at 227,000 for the mid-second century, while MacMullen reckons the total for the Severan period to have been 175,000.[4]

We might then turn to the question posed by MacMullen in 1980: 'How Big was the Roman Imperial Army?'[5] He demonstrated how many and varied had been the answers, quoting estimates of 500,000 for the second century, 420,000 under Marcus Aurelius, and 400,000 or 300,000 under Severus. His own preference for the latter period was 345,000. One of the more recent forays into this field was by Anthony Birley: he rejected lower estimates in favour of a figure for the mid-160s of 415-445,000.[6]

Even accepting the lower end of the scale of possibilities, it is worth remembering that few other examples of standing armies of anything approaching a third of a million men would be known until the 19th century.

Before turning to consider how this army of the first and second centuries developed and changed, it is worth noting that it always included remarkable examples of stability and longevity. David Kennedy has recently shown how the proportion of survival from the early to the later army varies widely from region to region: very few pre-Severan auxiliary units, for example, survive on the Rhine and Danube (fewer than 9%), whereas the proportion in Britain is 30% and rises to nearly 36% in the East.[7] Jones lists a whole series of examples of continuity into the early Byzantine period,[8] among which the stories of two legions are particularly striking. V Macedonica, probably raised in 43 BC, was still serving under Justinian (the unit thus surviving for some 600 years), while the last clear reference to a legion in battle occurs in the account by Theophylact Simocatta of the death of a soldier from the legion IV Parthica, then stationed at Beroe in Syria, on the field at Solachon.[9] That battle took place in the spring of 586 in the reign of Maurice – IV Parthica was then nearly 290 years old.

The Development of a Field Army: Early Precedents

One of the significant ways in which the army of the Later Empire was a different creature from that of the Early Empire was its division into frontier garrison forces and strategic reserve or field army units. The army of the Principate had no true reserve capacity, and

---

[1] Dr Brian Dobson, 'The Empire' in **Warfare in the Ancient World**, edited by General Sir John Hackett, London, 1989, pages 192-221, page 198.
[2] Eric Birley, 'Septimius Severus and the Roman Army' in **Epigraphische Studien** 8 (1969), pages 63-82, reprinted in M.P. Speidel (ed.), **The Roman Army: Papers 1929-1986 = Mavors: Roman Army Researches Volume 4**, Amsterdam, 1988, pages 21-40.
[3] Ramsay MacMullen, 'How Big was the Roman Imperial Army?', **Klio**, Band 62 (1980), Berlin, pages 451-460.
[4] Dobson, loc. cit. (note 1) and MacMullen, op. cit., page 452.
[5] Ibid.
[6] A.R. Birley, 'The Economic Effects of Roman Frontier Policy' in Anthony King and Martin Henig [edd.], **The Roman West in the Third Century: Contributions from Archaeology and History**, BAR International Series 109 (i), Oxford, 1981, pages 39-53.
[7] David Kennedy, 'The East' in John Wacher (ed.), **The Roman World**, London, 1987, pages 266-300.
[8] A.H.M. Jones, **The Later Roman Empire 284-602: A Social, Economic and Administrative Survey**, Oxford, 1964, Volume 2, page 655.
[9] Theophylact Simocatta, (Universal) History, translated with introduction and notes as **The History of Theophylact Simocatta** by Michael & Mary Whitby, Oxford, 1986.

much of the military history of the first and early second centuries involves the shuffling of forces between threatened fronts or areas of planned conquest.

In the early days of the Empire, the only real reserve forces under central command were the nine quingenary cohorts of the Praetorian Guard. However at first only three of these units (a mere 1,500 men) were stationed in Rome itself; the other six (4,500 troops) normally being scattered through various Italian cities, until Tiberius concentrated the Guard in Rome. It is difficult to support the view, put forward for example by Eric Birley,[10] that the four Urban cohorts and seven cohorts of vigiles should also be included as 'GHQ forces.' In practice they equate rather more comfortably to modern emergency rather than armed services: the vigiles, for example, carried no weapons.[11]

With such limited central reserve capacity available, it was therefore possible to deal with strategic crises only by either the use of detachments or by the transfer of entire units, even legions. Thus, for example, when the revolt of Tacfarinas in Numidia proved difficult to suppress in the early 20s, the legion IX Hispana was temporarily transferred 1,600 kilometres [a thousand miles] from Pannonia. Similarly, when the Syrian legions proved unable to cope with the First Jewish Revolt in Nero's reign, the legion XV Apollinaris was transferred to the East from Pannonia, where it in turn was replaced by X Gemina from Spain. A British instance occurred in AD 83, when Agricola's British command was depleted of vexillations from the legions II Adiutrix, IX Hispana and XX Valeria Victrix for Domitian's Chattan War. Such vexillations were in effect ad hoc field armies, and the prototype for later developments.

Transfers of whole legions appear to have occurred for the last time under Marcus Aurelius, when II Adiutrix from Lower Pannonia and I Minervia from Lower Germany (together probably with V Macedonica from Lower Moesia) were transferred east for the Parthian War of the early 160s. Thereafter the only permanent transfers seem to have been when V Macedonica moved to Dacia in 166, and finally when Dacia was abandoned in 270 and V Macedonica and XIII Gemina were withdrawn.

Although the emergence of a field army was a process rather than an event, one turning-point which has been considered to mark the development of a quasi-permanent de facto field army is the reign of Marcus Aurelius. The Danubian Wars of the late 160s and 170s exposed the weakness of the Imperial defences: Marcus's response to the crisis included the improvising of field armies and the raising of two new legions (II and III Italicae) for the protection of northern Italy.

The reign of Septimius Severus (AD 193-211) seems however to have been even more crucial in the history of the development of the army of the Later Empire. Severus inherited thirty legions, which he increased to 33 with the raising of I-III Parthicae. Although I and III Parthicae were stationed in the new province of Mesopotamia, II Parthica formed part of what can be seen as the greatly increased garrison of Rome – the Imperial bodyguard. This now comprised ten miliary cohorts of the reformed Praetorian Guard (10,000), 1,000 equites singulares and the new legion II Parthica (presumably about 5,000): a total of 16,000 men – or about three times the previous garrison. There also seem to have been available as central reserve elements Moorish javelin-men and Osrhoenian archers, stationed in the castra peregrina near the city. These latter forces are recorded being used as field army units under Alexander and Maximinus, and even as early as in AD 213 under Caracalla in Germany. It would seem reasonable therefore to see the reign of Severus as a vital stage: Eric Birley quoted with approval the description of these developments by Platnauer as representing the formation of 'the nucleus of a centralized field army.'[12]

Birley further draws attention to the raising at this time of a number of new auxiliary units, many based in Eastern provinces,[13] and to the creation of large, mobile forces of at least a semi-permanent nature. Examples of the latter are the exercitus Illyricus commanded by Ti. Claudius Candidus in the Asian, Parthian and Gallic expeditions;[14] the exerciti [sic] Mysiaci

---

[10] Eric Birley, op. cit. (note 2).
[11] Cf. Lawrence Keppie, **The Making of the Roman Army: From Republic to Empire**, London, 1984, page 188 and G.R. Watson, **The Roman Soldier**, London, 1969, page 19.
[12] Eric Birley, op. cit. (note 2).
[13] *Cohors I Septimia Belgarum* (Upper Germany), *ala II Septimia Syrorum* (Carnuntum), *cohors XX Palmyrenorum* (Dura), *Cohors IX Maurorum* (Mesopotamia) and possibly *cohors XII Palaestinorum* (Dura), *cohors IV Palaestinorum* (N.D. Or. 34, 46) and *cohors VIII Palmyrenorum* (N.D. Or. 31, 49).
[14] PIR^2 C 823.

which L. Marius Maximus led at Byzantium against Niger and at Lugdunum against Albinus;[15] and the task force from four German legions which served firstly under Claudius Gallus in the Second Parthian War[16] and later under C. Julius Septimius Castinus against 'defectores et rebelles'.[17]

Gallienus

Gallienus (sole emperor AD 260-268) faced a critical situation. His father, Valerian, had been captured by the Persian King, Shapur, who threatened the Eastern frontier; Postumus had formed a breakaway Gallic Empire that embraced also Germany, Britain and Spain; and the Alamanni were posing a serious threat to Raetia and even Italy.

As long ago as 1903, Ritterling (in his paper 'On the Roman Military Organisation of the Latter Part of the Third Century') drew attention to the importance of the poorly recorded reign of Gallienus to the development of a field army. This included a significant strengthening of the reserve cavalry forces: new elements were recruited from Dalmatian, Moorish and Osrhoenian auxiliaries; detached legionary cavalry (equites promoti);[18] scutarii (presumably 'shield bearers'); equites sagitarii (horse archers); and equites stablesiani (perhaps mounted legionaries or former provincial governors' cavalry guards).[19]

A similar growth of mobile infantry units can be detected at this time. This was the result of detaching vexillations from the frontier legions on an essentially permanent basis. Such a task force of British and German legions is recorded near Belgrade, and pia fidelis coin issues struck in 259-60 honour Rhine and Danube legionary vexillations based in north Italy.[20] Epigraphic evidence similarly attests the presence of elements of II Parthica and III Augusta in north-west Macedonia; German and British vexillations at Sirmium in Pannonia; and detachments of two Dacian and probably four Pannonian legions at Poetovio.

By the 260s therefore a substantial de facto field army was in existence, comprising infantry formations based on vexillations from frontier legions and cavalry units, many of which were newly raised.

Diocletian

Although precedents for a field army can be traced back into the early first century and particularly to the developments under Severus and Gallienus, the traditional interpretation remains valid in the sense that the ultimate form of the Imperial Army with a de jure field army was principally the work of Diocletian and Constantine in the late third and early fourth centuries.

The Christian critic, Lactantius, writing quite soon after the event, is often said to have accused Diocletian of having quadrupled the army. In fact it is far from clear that this is what Lactantius meant and it should be noted that his use of the verb 'contenderent' itself implies striving for larger forces rather than implying success in such an endeavour.[21] A quadrupling in any case is inherently implausible: John Casey, for example, has suggested a more convincing increase at this period of about a third – to something like the oddly precise 435,266 claimed by John Lydus in the mid-sixth century.[22]

It is generally agreed that Diocletian inherited 33 legions (including the three relatively new ones raised by Severus) and then substantially increased this total. Although Parker[23] thought the number of Diocletianic creations may have been no more than about 17, a higher figure is

---

[15] **ILS** 2935.
[16] **A.E.** 1957, 123.
[17] **PIR**² I 566.
[18] The *equites promoti* are not attested until the very late third century. Even if **all** legionary cavalry elements were at full strength and **all** were detached to the field army, fewer than 4,000 troopers would have been raised (33 x 120 = 3,960). It might also be asked: Why should the legions suddenly cease all need for scouts and couriers in the third century?
[19] It needs to be considered in this context whether Severus' substantial increase in the number of provinces (to about fifty) does not imply a similar increase in the quantity of governors' bodyguards. The number of provinces was of course increased again later: there were over 100 from Diocletian's time.
[20] Cf. Roger Tomlin, 'The Late-Roman Empire' in General Sir John Hackett (ed.), **Warfare in the Ancient World**, London, 1989, page 223.

[21] [Lucius Caecilius Firmianus] Lactantius, **De Mortibus Persecutorum**, 7, 2, edited and translated by J.L. Creed, Oxford, 1984. Lactantius, who may have been an African and lived from *c*. AD 240/5 to *c*. 320/5, was probably writing in *c*. AD 314/315.
[22] John Casey, **The Legions in the Later Roman Empire: The Fourth Annual Caerleon Lecture**, Caerleon, 1991, page 12. Lydus's statistic may be a genuine official figure: he had after all worked in the office of the Praetorian Prefect, Zoticus, in Constantinople from *c*. AD 511, originally as an *exceptor* or 'speedwriter'.
[23] H.M.D. Parker, 'The Legions of Diocletian and Constantine' in **J.R.S.**, 23, London, 1933, pages 175-189.

usually proposed: Nischer[24] suggested 34 and Casey 36 or 37.[25] Tomlin's 'doubled'[26] seems an acceptable compromise: from 33 to approximately 66 legions.

Most legions appear to have been posted in pairs to the frontiers. There is no indisputable evidence on the size of the new legions, or indeed of legions in general at this point but documentary and archaeological indications of new, smaller legions will be examined later. It is worth noting that the raising of 33 new legions of traditional (5,000) strength would have required the recruitment in a short period of some 165,000 extra legionaries; 1,000-strong legions – a widely accepted concept now for new formations at least – would have needed only 33,000 recruits.[27] The sheer implausibility of the former figure is perhaps one of the strongest reasons for needing to assume legions of a substantially reduced establishment by the early fourth century. By contrast, the previous largest number of legions raised at the same time would have been the three legions Parthicae formed by Severus probably in c. AD 197.[28]

The legions, in any case, should perhaps by this time no longer be regarded as the élite frontier troops of the army: this rôle was now taken by field army cavalry detachments or vexillationes, which served alongside some traditional alae and cohortes.

Diocletian significantly strengthened the field army. This now included two new legions (Ioviani and Herculiani), which had originally been Danubian units equipped with the martiobarbulus;[29] new élite legions, like the Solenses and Martenses; the Lanciarii (originating in lance-equipped Praetorians and legionaries[30]); and crack cavalry units, such as the scholae, equites comites and equites promoti (these latter being formed from detachments of provincial bodyguards and Praetorian cavalry).

This mobile reserve remained relatively small with only a small proportion retained centrally and, to meet particular emergencies, had to be reinforced by ad hoc detachments from the frontier legionary garrisons: Tomlin,[31] for example, quotes an Egyptian papyrus of 295 which records some ten pairs of legionary vexillations.

Constantine

It has been stated that '. . . (the) Emperor Constantine was the innovator who created the army of the later Empire'[32] and, although debate will no doubt continue as to how significant were the foundations laid by his predecessors, it is probably true that this reign (306–337) saw the apogee of the Imperial army.

Following his victory at the Milvian Bridge in 312 (and apparently developing a concept originating under Constantius or Maximian), Constantine established new infantry élite units called auxilia: these included the Cornuti ('horned men'), Bracchiati ('armlet wearers'), Iovii and Victores. These units seem to have been raised largely among Rhineland and Gallic settler Germans (laeti). They have been described as the 'shock troops of the late-Roman army.'[33]

Following the example of Diocletian, Constantine did raise some new legions[34] but a more important development was the establishment of new mobile infantry units (also called 'legiones') formed from permanently detached elements of the frontier legions and other strategic garrisons: these could retain an old-style legionary title (like V Macedonica), or a numerical title (such as Primani or Secundani), or a geographical title (like the Tungrecani).

Mainly due to their support of Maxentius, Constantine disbanded the Praetorians and equites singulares Augusti: partly to replace

---

[24] E. Nischer, 'The Army Reforms of Diocletian and Constantine and their modifications up to the time of the Notitia Dignitatum' in **J.R.S.**, 13, London, 1923.
[25] John Casey, loc. cit. (note 22).
[26] Roger Tomlin, 'The Mobile Army' in Peter Connolly (ed.) **Greece and Rome at War**, London, 1981, pages 249–259. Some 15 of the suggested new legions can be identified as definitely Diocletianic.
[27] By contrast (and in addition) an army of some 300,000 men would require about 12,000 new recruits per annum to replace natural wastage, assuming annual retirement of 4% of total strength. (Roger Tomlin [**pers. comm.**] suggests that the real level may have been about twice as high as a result of a lower life expectancy.)
[28] Cf. J.C. Mann, **Legionary Recruitment and Veteran Settlement during the Principate**, Insitute of Archaeology Occasional Publications No. 7, London, 1983.
[29] This has been translated (e.g. by Roger Tomlin, [1989], page 227) as a 'weighted dart'.

[30] Cf. Tomlin, loc. cit..
[31] Op. cit. [1981], page 251.
[32] P. A. Holder, **The Roman Army in Britain**, London, 1982, page 97.
[33] Tomlin, loc. cit..
[34] Including those named after him such as *Secunda Flavia Constantiniana* (**N.D.** Oc. 5, 253).

them as Imperial 'Guard' units, new mobile cavalry formations were added to the field army. These included new units called scholae; vexillationes of cavalry; the mounted equivalent of auxilia such as the equites Cornuti; and units, like the Dalmatae and stablesiani, which seem to have been former field army units from the time of Gallienus posted to frontier garrisons and then re-mustered to the mobile reserves.

It has been argued that Constantine's reign saw the division of the field army into 'palatine' and 'comitatensian' unit types but the former expression is in fact first used only from the 360s, and it is far from clear in any case that these two appellations represented a clear demarcation between 'guard' and 'line' units. There also appear in the fourth century army units described as pseudocomitatenses: the Notitia, for example, records ten legiones pseudocomitatenses under the magister militum per Orientem, nine under the magister militum per Illyricum and 18 in the command of the magister militum Praesentalis.[35] One suggestion has been that these were not true mobile units but more probably frontier command detachments temporarily or permanently assigned to the field army but not accorded field army status or privileges.

Constantine's field army first seems to have been used in 312 against Maxentius in Italy, when units originally stationed in Britain, Germany and Gaul were deployed. Unlike the static, frontier garrisons, the field army units are listed without details of their bases in the Notitia. This is a reasonable reflection of reality: such forces had no fixed stations but were either on campaign or billeted in towns. Constantine created two new commanding generals for the cavalry and infantry field army formations: respectively, the magister equitum and the magister peditum. A later development, and presumably a reaction to events, was the creation of regional field armies – in Gaul, Illyricum, the East (with headquarters at Antioch), Africa, Britain, Spain and Thrace. Some of these regional mobile armies (at least) did not emerge until very late in the 4th century: the small command of the comes Britanniarum, for instance. It has been calculated[36] that by c.

AD 395 there were in existence about 325 field army units, divided very nearly equally between Western and Eastern Empires. It is perhaps surprising to note that these 'mobile' forces were predominantly infantry: only 85 units (26%) were mounted, giving a total reserve cavalry capacity for the whole Empire of perhaps only 17–34,000 men.[37]

Constantine must therefore have left a substantial proportion of the Imperial forces in the static units on the frontiers. These forces are represented in the Notitia by the 'below the line' elements in the Eastern commands and – exceptionally in the West – in the command of the dux Britanniarum (Oc. 40). Those troops actually serving in effect as frontier police (such as the Hadrian's Wall fort garrisons) are described as limitanei: these comprised the traditional alae and cohortes, as well as numeri. The frontier legions and new-style formations (cunei, equites, milites and auxilia) are classed as ripenses: it is not clear whether there was any real difference between ripenses and limitanei, or whether the former were in fact a type of the latter.

There remains considerable argument about the quality of these non-mobile elements of the Late Roman Empire. There are clear indications that they were less favourably treated than the mobile troops in terms of pay and equipment, and physical requirements also indicate that the frontier forces had a lower status.[38] Contrary to one line of argument however, there seems no evidence on the other hand that the frontier forces had declined to a type of peasant militia: the now well known account in Eugippius's vita Severini of the decline of Roman power in late fifth century Noricum includes the story of soldiers from cohors IX Batavorum unsuccessfully attempting to track down their arrears of pay. Although this incident occurred only a few years before the Batavians' fort at Passau fell to Hunumundus, the troops clearly still regarded themselves as regulars entitled to regular pay.

There are moreover a number of instances showing that the limitanei could serve perfectly satisfactorily as fighting troops. Tomlin[39] cites

---

[35] Respectively N.D. Or. 7, 28–58, Or. 9, 39–48 and Oc. 5, 256–274.
[36] By Tomlin, op. cit. [1989], page 236. For the development of smaller, regional field armies, see J.C. Mann, 'Power, Force and the Frontiers of the Empire' in J.R.S., 69, London, 1979, pages 175–183, especially page 182.
[37] Tomlin (ibid., page 238) says that cavalry units of the field army would have been 'much less than 500 men' strong. 85 regiments each 400 strong would have totalled 34,000 men; if they were only 200 strong, the total would have been just 17,000 troopers. Cf. also Chapter 4, note 81.
[38] See for example the Theodosian Code 7, 1, 18 and 7, 22, 2 (4).
[39] Op. cit. [1981], pages 253–4.

their contribution to the defence of Amida in 359 and to Julian's Persian expedition four years later. There also seem to have been occasions – Tomlin quotes one from 363 and another from the early fifth century[40] – when substantial numbers of limitanei were transformed into field army units (as pseudocomitatenses). Isaac has drawn attention to the use of limitanei by Belisarius in Mesopotamia and also that the term itself is not attested before AD 363.[41]

Irregular Forces

Some attention should perhaps now be given to an area that allows of even less precision than does consideration of the standing forces of the Empire, namely the matter of irregular troops. The origins of Rome's auxiliary troops is largely explained by a need to recruit non-citizens to cover contingencies not well provided for by Rome's own levies, such as light infantry and cavalry. Similarly, non-Imperial or allied forces are recorded as playing significant rôles in many campaigns throughout the Empire's history.

There are a number of literary references to Late Roman armies including large numbers of temporarily recruited non-Romans.[42] For example, Themistius mentions Armenians and Iberians serving in the 380s and under Stilicho but the Notitia has no record of such troops. In the same way, large numbers of Goths fought with Theodosius against Eugenius in AD 394 (10,000 were reported to have been killed) but the Notitia records only a handful of Gothic units.[43] The bulk of the Goths would therefore have been allied tribal formations[44] recruited for the duration and then demobilised; there would have been obvious financial advantages in such an arrangement.

An equally unclear picture is all we have of the local militias, whose rôle in the defence of the Later Empire must at times have been crucial. Eric Birley[45] has shown that such local militias were well established by the first century and figure, for example, on a number of occasions in the account of the events of AD 69 by Tacitus in The Histories.[46] In the 170s, Didius Julianus is reported as having raised militia forces in Belgica to cope with an invasion by the Chauci[47] and a little over half a century later Gallienus took similar measures in north Africa.[48] Birley even suggests that cohors I Cornoviorum, attested at Newcastle in the Notitia,[49] may have originated as a tribal militia organised in the first century perhaps to watch the Ordovices.

The existence of these shadowy and often unquantifiable additional military resources may well help to explain certain oddities of the Late Roman Army – such as the relatively small size of some recorded expeditionary forces (just 13,000 with Julian in Gaul in 357;[50] only four regiments sent to Britain with Theodosius in 367;[51] and Stilicho's African expeditionary force of 398 recorded by Claudian as comprising just six field army units[52]) and perhaps some apparent gaps in frontier defences, such as that in western Britain.

---

[40] Ibid..
[41] Benjamin Isaac, 'The Meaning of The Terms **Limes** and **Limitanei**' in **J.R.S.**, 78, London, 1988, pages 125-147.
[42] See J.H.G.W. Liebeschuetz, 'Generals, Federates and Bucellarii in Roman Armies Around AD 400' in Philip Freeman and David Kennedy [edd.], **The Defence of the Roman and Byzantine East: Proceedings of a Colloquium held at the University of Sheffield in April 1986**, BAR International Series 297, Oxford, 1986, pages 463-474, reprinted in **From Diocletian to the Arab Conquest: Change in the Late Roman Empire**, Aldershot, 1990 (19).
[43] Cf. Jordanes, **Get.** 145 and Orosius, **Historia contra paganos**, 7, 35. The **Notitia** records *cohors I Gothorum* (Or. 33, 32), *Teruingi* (Or. 6, 61) and *Visi* (Or. 5, 61).
[44] Liebeschuetz, op. cit. (note 42) regards these forces as mercenaries.

[45] Eric Birley, 'Local Militias in the Roman Empire' in **Bonner Historia-Augusta-Colloquium 1972/1974**, Bonn, 1976, pages 65-73, reprinted in **Mavors 4, Roman Army Researches Volume 4**, Amsterdam, 1988, pages 387-394.
[46] Such as 1, 67; 1, 68; 3, 5; and 2, 58.
[47] **SHA**, Vita Didii Juliani, 1, 7.
[48] Ibid., Vita Gallieni, 13, 8 and an inscription from Saldae (modern Bejaia/Bougie in Algeria) [= **A.E.**, 1928, 38].
[49] **N.D.** Oc. 40, 34.
[50] This was however one of only two armies in Gaul at that time intended to form a pincer movement: the other army (under Barbatio, *magister peditum*) comprised another 25,000 troops from Italy. It was planned for this joint force of 38,000 to trap the 35,000 Alamanni under Chnodomar and Serapio.
[51] There must also have been an issue of the availability of maritime transport, which in such emergency conditions may well have limited numbers that could be transferred, for example, to Britain.
[52] Claudian lists the *Herculiani seniores, Ioviani seniores, Nervii, Felices iuniores, Augusti* and *Leones iuniores* (**In Gildonem** 418-423).

Britain

The direct evidence relating to the changed Roman Army of the later Empire and the provinces of Britain is limited. It seems however safe to assert initially that there seems little dispute that the British garrison was reduced, perhaps sharply, from an earlier peak.

At the higher end of the range of possibilities for the mid-second century, one estimate would put the Roman forces in Brtain just in excess of 50,000 men.[53] Although this might be somewhat high, it is unlikely to be excessively so and the hard evidence of the O-Szöny diploma of AD 122[54] can be read without undue speculation as implying a garrison at that point of rather more than 45,000 (on paper, at least).[55] This would incidentally suggest that some 13% of the total Imperial forces were then stationed in Britain: not merely the largest provincial army but also about 40% larger than the next largest (those of Dacia and Syria).[56]

It seems likely that a major factor (if not **the** major factor) in explaining the reduction of the British garrison from perhaps 45–50,000 men in AD 120–150 down to a size in c. AD 400 variously estimated at 33,500,[57] 28,000,[58] 20,000,[59] 14,000[60] or even just 12,000[61] was the relatively quiescent nature of the previously troublesome northern frontier during the third century. While the Rhine, Danube, Eastern and North African frontiers all provided crises of a greater or lesser importance, in contrast northern Britain for the 85 years at least from 211 to 296 was largely peaceful.

A hard-pressed central government would have been short-sighted not to have begun to look upon the British garrison as a wasting asset and ready source of reinforcements for more critical sectors: '... Britain's large army was one which could safely be siphoned of troops, whilst leaving sufficient to safeguard the island.'[62]

Temporary detachments had of course a long history and may even have been the norm, at least on a localised scale in the first and second centuries: a well-known instance is the despatch of a vexillation of legio IX Hispana to serve with Domitian against the Chatti in AD 83.[63] This pattern continued into the third century with a vexillation of legio XX recorded at Mainz in AD 255, at which point a detachment of II Augusta (possibly including its 7th Cohort) was also absent from headquarters.[64] The delightful roundel or badge of Aurelius Cervianus apparently commemorating an officer serving with a task force of the IInd and XXth legions, which was presumably in Gaul en route to the Rhine or Danube, is usually dated to the mid-third century also.[65] Shortly afterwards, however (apparently in AD 260), a joint force of presumably IInd and XXth legionaries[66] appeared on the Danube in Pannonia. It seems more likely than not that these cohorts were cut off from their parent units by the rebellion of Postumus and the creation of his breakaway Gallic Empire and never returned: it seems inconceivable that Gallienus's 'legitimate' central government would allow a revolt to be reinforced from areas under its own control.[67]

Although this is generally assumed to mark the early stages of a development which saw

---

[53] A.R. Birley, op. cit. (note 6).
[54] **CIL** 16 69.
[55] The diploma records: ten quingenary alae (5,120), a milliary ala (768), 35 quingenary cohorts (16,800) and two milliary cohorts (1,600) = 24,288. If the diploma can be assumed to include some 3/4 of the garrison, this would bring the total of auxiliaries to some 30,000. Allowing 15,000 for the three legions gives a grand total of about 45,000.
[56] Based on the figures in A.R. Birley, op. cit. (note 6). Might one factor influencing the development of such a large British garrison be the need to have substantial forces available in a province that was an island and could therefore only be reinforced relatively slowly?
[57] A.H.M. Jones, **The Later Roman Empire 284-602: A Social, Economic and Administrative Survey**, Oxford, 1964, Volume 3, page 380.
[58] David Breeze, 'Demand and Supply on the Northern Frontier' in RogerMiket and Colin Burgess [edd.], **Between and Beyond the Walls: Essays on the Prehistory and History of North Britain in Honour of George Jobey**, Edinburgh, 1984, pages 264-286. This figure includes a 15% reduction from Breeze's claimed theoretical total of 33,000 'to bring them into line with the more realistic actual totals suggested by most army documents.'
[59] Simon James, 'Britain and the Late Roman Army' in T.F.C. Blagg and A.C. King [edd.], **Military and Civilian in Roman Britain**, BAR British Series 136, Oxford, 1984, Chapter 7 (pages 161-186).
[60] David Breeze, op. cit. (note 58), with unit sizes reduced to take account of Duncan-Jones's proposals.
[61] Simon James, op. cit. (note 59): the lower end of his range of possibilities.

[62] Simon Esmonde Cleary, 'Constantine I to Constantine III' in Malcolm Todd (ed.), **Research on Roman Britain: 1960-89**, Britannia Monograph Series No. 11, London, 1989, pages 235-244. A modern parallel might be with the British Army of the Rhine and its effective use as a reserve force available for contingencies such as Ulster and the Gulf War.
[63] **ILS** 1025.
[64] **CIL** 13 6780 (legio XX at Mainz), and **RIB** 334 (rebuilding at Caerleon in 255/260).
[65] The distinctive round shields suggest such a date.
[66] **CIL** 3 3228. This was possibly the same 'task force' serving on the Rhine some five years earlier.
[67] The **Notitia** records a number of field army units which might originate from vexillations of II Augusta.

Change and Development in the Later Empire

significant withdrawals of elements of the British garrison perhaps even as late as the early fifth century, there is in fact very little explicit evidence to support this not implausible scenario. Under Carausius and Allectus, for example, some movement of troops to the Continent might well seem more than likely but no positive proof for such movement is available.

The assumption that units of the British garrison were withdrawn to support Magnentius and either destroyed at the battle of Mursa in AD 351 or disbanded after that defeat (or kept on the Continent) is similarly quite likely but not susceptible to proof.

Although some have suggested otherwise, there is no reason to suppose troop withdrawals in or after the 'barbarian conspiracy' of 367 occurred, although the reinforcements recorded were no doubt of an emergency nature. Units may well have been destroyed in battle that year or have disintegrated in the apparent chaos that followed but it is equally possible that the small size of the expeditionary force sent to recover Britain (just four field army regiments) may partly reflect the fact that the British garrison remained largely in being, if less than intact. It is also worth recalling that 'There is no archaeological evidence from any Wall fort for destruction by enemy action.'[68] It has been argued on the other hand that the old third century garrison of Britain was deliberately run down from c. AD 275–300 and that, for example, some elements in the earlier part of the Notitia list for the Duke of Britain represented field army drafts posted to this country probably in c. AD 367/373.[69]

It has become a relatively common assumption, too, that when Magnus Maximus made his bid for the Imperial throne in the 380s this must also have involved withdrawals from the army of Britain and this is frequently quantified to include specifically, for example, legio XX Valeria Victrix from Chester and perhaps the Seguntienses from Caernarvon and the limitanei units from the north-west and Wales, together possibly with some Wall fort garrisons and perhaps even legio VI Victrix from York.[70] There is a great need for caution here however because '... like alleged withdrawals by earlier usurpers, the evidence is extremely thin.'[71] Not only is it difficult to link archaeological evidence of the apparent abandonment of a particular fort to a narrowly defined historical event but such abandonment could represent transfer of a unit within the province rather than outside. It is also worth remembering that Maximus has in the past been held responsible for the final evacuation of the Wall but numismatic and pottery evidence have since clearly revealed continued occupation well after the 380s.

Although we have some literary sources for the period relating to the activities of Stilicho in the late 390s and early 400s, the picture that emerges is far from clear. The court poet, Claudian, appears to refer to military success against Scots, Picts and Saxons[72] but it is by no means evident whether this involved more than naval victories or whether reinforcements were sent or whether Stilicho himself was personally committed. On the other hand, Claudian provides us with perhaps the sole unambiguous reference to troop withdrawals:

'venit et extremis legio praetenta Britannis, quae Scoto dat frena truci ferroque notatas, perlegit exsangues Picto moriente figuras.'[73]

The mention of a legion and apparent description of northern Britain make a link with VI Victrix at York difficult to avoid but there is reason for caution in jumping too readily to conclusions not necessarily supported by Claudian's words, where convention or lack of interest in military technicalities or even the needs of metre may have to be considered.

Ingenious attempts have been made to connect Claudian's references to the events of c. AD 395–402 to the even more obscure and confused story recounted in chapters 14–19 of Gildas's de excidio Britonum.[74] Gildas does indeed describe two Roman expeditions sent to Britain some time between the death of Maximus (383) and the famous appeal to Aëtius

---

[68] Nicholas Hodgson, 'The Notitia Dignitatum and the later Roman garrison of Britain' in Valerie A. Maxfield and Michael J. Dobson, **Roman Frontier Studies 1989: Proceedings of the XVth International Congress of Roman Frontier Studies**, Exeter, 1991, pages 84–92.
[69] Ibid.
[70] See for example Malcolm Todd, **Roman Britain 55 BC – AD 400**, Glasgow, 1981, pages 235–236; Sheppard Frere, **Britannia**, London, 1967, pages 234–235; P.A. Holder, op. cit. (note 32), page 19; and Simon James, op. cit. (note 59).
[71] Peter Salway, **Roman Britain**, The Oxford History of England 1A, Oxford, 1981, page 403.
[72] Claudian, **On the Consulship of Stilicho**, delivered early 400.
[73] Claudian, **De Bello Getico**, AD 416/418 referring to AD 401/402.
[74] For example, by Peter Salway, op. cit. (note 71), pages 419–424.

(446/454?) and two barbarian wars, one specifically involving Scots and Picts, the other perhaps implicitly so. Gildas was no historian and his purposes were not historical but the basic outline of his account is not inherently implausible (even if it does include the famous reference to the building of a turf wall trans insulam!)[75] and may indeed be a muddled account of Stilicho's British policies, including troop withdrawals. Little further certainty is available from what is after all a work of religious denunciation not historical scholarship and which contains no dates and only about a dozen non-Biblical personal names.

Ironically, it seems more than likely that, even if he were responsible for troop withdrawals, Stilicho also had the garrison of Britain reinforced. The Notitia records a small field army of nine units (six cavalry and three infantry) under a comes Britanniarum[76] which may represent part of a reorganisation under Stilicho in c. AD 395. The fact that one of the regiments is named after the western emperor Honorius makes it difficult to date the establishment of the Count's command earlier than 395.[77]

Moving towards the end of Roman control in Britain, the reign of Constantine III (407-411) has traditionally been seen as marking the final, catastrophic withdrawal of Imperial forces from the island. This has been argued not just in terms of the need for the usurpation to be made secure with drafts of the British garrison being shipped to Gaul in 407 but also from the appearance in the field army of the Gallic magister equitum of units apparently taken from the Saxon Shore - the Secundani Britones, Abulci, and Exploratores.[78] Even if these identifications are correct, there are many anomalies in the Notitia of this sort, and even if temporary withdrawals did occur we '... have no evidence that ... (they) were not made up after the initial successes of Constantine's régime.'[79]

Logic then suggests that the very large British garrison of the mid-second century must have been greatly reduced in size during the third and fourth centuries and, as we have seen, some quite precise attempts have been made to quantify that assumption. Direct evidence is however lacking beyond the 250s and 260s, and it would be appropriate therefore to establish whether indirect evidence can provide a clearer picture.

Michael Fulford, in his 1989 paper,[80] attempted to examine whether coin or pottery evidence demonstrated any trends. Arguing that the import of Gaulish sigillata shows a marked decline from perhaps c. AD 225 onwards, Fulford links this to military expenditure and claims that the decline of spending on high quality imported goods must show either that 'expensive overseas contracts [sc. were] terminated but that the size of the army ... remained the same or that the volume of goods required had fallen because of reductions in the military establishment.'[81] Fulford favours the latter explanation and supports this with the claim that internal trade involving the military - especially pottery for the northern frontier - also shows a decline.

On the other hand Fulford points out that the decline of bronze supplies pre-dates the Severan campaigns, when military forces might be expected to have been at peak strength. Coin evidence is equally inconclusive both due to the debasement of the early third century and to the increasing significance of remuneration to the troops in kind through the annona militaris.

Reductions in accommodation in barracks with the building of some barrack blocks in the fourth century as individual 'chalets' for family units has been seen at various forts, especially on Hadrian's Wall, and this has led to calculations of reduced garrisons, in some cases greatly reduced. This issue will be further examined in chapter 5, where it will be seen that the whole 'chalet' concept has come under attack and may not provide the evidence for very small Late Empire units that was once thought.

Another example of the difficult nature of archaeological evidence in this area comes with the thesis that in the late third and early fourth centuries (from perhaps c. AD 270) a number of forts on Hadrian's Wall or in its hinterland were greatly run down or even abandoned, to be re-occupied with new units perhaps under Constantius. This situation has been claimed, for example, to have existed at Haltonchesters, Rudchester, South Shields, Bowness-on-

---

[75] Gildas, **De Excidio Britonum**, 15, 3.
[76] **N.D.** Oc. 7, 154-156 and 200-205.
[77] Viz. **Equites Honoriani Seniores** (N.D. 7, 202). Some would even date the establishment of this command late in the regency of Stilicho or even to the usurpation of Constantine III - i.e., late in the first or very early in the second decade of the fifth century.
[78] Ibid. 7, 84, 109 and 110.
[79] Peter Salway, op. cit. (note 71), page 429.

[80] Michael Fulford, 'The Economy of Roman Britain' in Malcolm Todd (ed.), op. cit. (note 62), pages 175-201.
[81] Ibid.

Solway and Birdoswald.[82] A contrary case[83] has argued that the lack of epigraphic and numismatic evidence is a general rather than a local phenomenon, and that an apparent layer of humus in some third century buildings at Rudchester, Haltonchesters and Birdoswald may not be evidence of abandonment but of occupation with a certain decline of military order. This in turn may result from a sort of semi-autonomy forced on many forts by (a) the lack of coinage reaching the frontiers and (b) the cessation of the old practice of sending equites from other provinces to serve as auxiliary commanders: the latter custom must evidently have been at least interrupted with the establishment of the Gallic Empire.

None of the above amounts to proof that the overall size of the British garrison did not decline nor that individual units did not become smaller but does indicate some of the problems involved in proving or at least quantifying the case.

As far as the legions are concerned, the epigraphic evidence will not take us beyond the middle of the third century. There is a possible tile-stamp recording II Augusta in 269/71; otherwise it disappears from the epigraphic records in 255/60.[84] VI Victrix is last recorded a little earlier, in 238/44 or perhaps slightly later.[85] XX Valeria Victrix is just possibly recorded on a tile-stamp of 249/51[86] and milites from the legion dedicated an altar at Milecastle 52 at Bankshead in 262/6.[87]

Carausius's coin series record both II Augusta and XX Valeria Victrix in the period 287/93 but not the VIth Legion. On the other hand, the Notitia – perhaps a record of the situation as late as the late fourth century or even slightly later – includes II Augusta and VI Victrix but not XX Valeria Victrix. The Twentieth's fortress at Chester shows little sign of military occupation much beyond c. AD 300 in any case. Although the bases of the other two legions is less than clear in the Notitia, there is no good reason not still to place VI Victrix in York in the fourth century while II Augusta may have moved from Caerleon to Richborough as early as the 270s, although it has been recently argued that its Notitia HQ was in fact in London.[88]

Two areas in which a relatively clear picture emerges are Wales and the forts beyond Hadrian's Wall. With regard to the former, Jeffrey Davies puts the peak occupation in c. AD 80 at three legions and probably 35 or 36 (but perhaps as many as 38–40) auxiliary units: a total of approximately 20,000 auxiliaries.[89] This was however very short-lived and by c. AD 138 had been greatly reduced, comprising no more than seven sites by c. AD 300.[90] A gradual decline continued until by c. AD 394 the only sites likely still to have been occupied were Caerwent (possibly a field army base?) and Carmarthen (where the evidence consists of just a single coin). Traditional dates for the abandonment of the northern outpost forts have been in the 360s or preferably c. 342/3 (in connection with the visit of Constans and based on the complete absence of the common Period 23 coins of Constantine II) but many would now argue for an even earlier date of c. AD 312/14, following Constantine's visit.[91]

The British sections of the Notitia record only five alae, 18 cohorts and five numeri which are clearly survivals from the third century. Although this represents well over half the non-legionary garrison units recorded in the Notitia, there had evidently been an influx of 'new' units to Britain probably from the last quarter of the third century.

The defeat of the Gallic Empire in 274 probably saw a substantial influx of new units, such as the equites Dalmatae (one of many such regiments raised by Gallienus[92]) and the numerus Directorum, which were stationed behind Hadrian's Wall as a mobile reserve or on the Saxon Shore. Other reinforcements probably

---

[82] By, for example, David J. Breeze and Brian Dobson, 'Roman Military Deployment in North England' in **Britannia** 16, London, 1985, pages 1–19.
[83] R.F.J. Jones, 'Change on the Frontier: Northern Britain in the Third Century' in Anthony King and Martin Henig [edd.], op. cit. (note 6), pages 393–414.
[84] **RIB** 334.
[85] **RIB** 583.
[86] **E.E.**, 9, 1274a, b and **RIB** 452.
[87] **RIB** 1956.

[88] Nicholas Fuentes, 'Fresh thoughts on the Saxon Shore' in Valerie A. Maxfield and Michael J. Dobson [edd.], op. cit. (note 68), pages 58–64.
[89] Jeffrey L. Davies, 'Soldiers, peasants and markets in Wales and the Marches' in BAR 136, op. cit., pages 93–127 and 'Roman military deployment in Wales and the Marches from Pius to Theodosius' in Maxfield and Dobson, op. cit. (note 68), pages 52–57.
[90] Caernarvon, Caersws, Brecon Gaer (probably at a very reduced level), Castell Collen (probably only until c. AD 310), Forden Gaer, Loughor and Caerhun.
[91] Nicholas Hodgson, op. cit. (note 68), pages 84–92, identified Axelodunum as Netherby and therefore claimed one outpost was still occupied at the end of the fourth century.
[92] The appellation 'Dalmatian' may refer to units long based in that area, rather than originally raised there (cf. legion IX Hispana).

arrived with Constantius in c. AD 297+: the ala Herculea (a creation of the period 295/305), stationed at Elslack according to the Notitia, may have been one such unit. The process presumably continued in some piecemeal form during the early fourth century, as evidenced by the presence at Danum (Doncaster?) in the Notitia of another mobile reserve unit, the equites Crispiani which presumably could not have been created before AD 317.[93]

A number of new style, Late Army units probably arrived in Britain in the aftermath of the crisis of AD 367. Holder[94] cites seven possible permanent reinforcement regiments from that period: the milites Tungrecani and the numeri Defensorum, Fortensium, Nerviorum Dictensium, Pacensium, Solensium and Turnacensium. These units were also distributed as garrisons for northern and Saxon Shore forts. It is perhaps in this context that Ammianus relates the appointment in 372 of a German prince, Fraomar, to the command of 'a large and powerful contingent' of Alamanni in Britain.[95]

Attempts have been made to create an impression of the state of the Roman Army in Britain in the last twenty-thirty years of the fourth century by assuming the British sections of the Notitia to date from then and combining its evidence with that of archaeology for other sites occupied then. Stephen Johnson, for example, tried such an exercise for northern Britain.[96] The Notitia lists 35 forts under the command of the dux Britanniarum, 17 along Hadrian's Wall and 18 behind it. To these Johnson adds: 12 forts probably occupied in the 370s but not in the Notitia, four newly built fourth century forts, two legionary fortresses, four forts possibly occupied, three fortlets and six signal stations.[97] In addition to this large northern border command, the maritime defence command of the Saxon Shore included some nine units (with possibly ten stations), and there was also the regional field army of the comes Britanniarum. To these can perhaps also be added urban militia forces and whatever defences there must surely have been – albeit unrecorded – for the west of Britain.

It may be therefore that, even allowing for intermittent withdrawal of troops, a much smaller size for most units and possible inaccuracies and obsolete elements in the Notitia, the shadow at least of an impressive force remained in Britain at the close of the fourth century. As with other aspects of Roman rule – the villa economy, urban life, the upkeep of roads and the Imperial post – the garrison, with its dependence on the existence of Imperial rule for its recruitment, training, officering and payment, can hardly have long survived the break with the Continent in c. AD 409–11. This need imply nothing about the behaviour of individual soldiers or even units (as the story of IX Batavorum at Passau shows) but the structure per se must have collapsed quite suddenly in the second decade of the fifth century AD.

The coinage record allows us to glimpse something of what must have happened. Bronze coins down to the numerous SALVS REIPVBLICAE issues from Rome and Aquileia struck in 395+ did reach Britain in quantity but the later VRBS ROMA FELIX type of c. AD 403/4 and subsequent GLORIA ROMANORVM issue of Honorius from Arles and Lyons are not found. This implies quite clearly that the central government ceased sending official salary payments (and presumably replacement military and civilian officials) in approximately AD 402. Silver coins later than c. 400 are unusual and gold coins are not found from beyond 403.

---

[93] Roger Tomlin (**pers. comm.**) suggests that this cavalry regiment could have been named instead after Crispianum in Pannonia.
[94] Op. cit. (note 32), pages 131–132. This is a very speculative list.
[95] Ammianus Marcellinus, **Histories**, 29, 4, 7.
[96] In **Later Roman Britain**, London, 1980, Map 4, page 25.
[97] And 17 defended towns.

CHAPTER 3

THE ARMY IN PEACE AND WAR: LITERARY EVIDENCE

As the British examples cited in Chapter 2 exemplify,[1] the epigraphic record is generally poorer in quantity and quality by the mid-third century. Similarly, it would be a reasonable generalisation that the army of the Late Empire is relatively poorly served by the literary evidence when contrasted for example with the detailed account Tacitus provides for the period AD 14-70. The opening part of the Annals, which deals with the Rhine-Danube mutinies and Germanicus's German campaigns in the opening year of Tiberius's reign, alone includes references to ten legions[2] and specified quantities of auxiliaries.[3]

With some exceptions, the literary record for the fourth and fifth centuries does not provide this level of detail, which in the case of the surviving works of Tacitus would allow reasonably full unit histories to be compiled for the legions at least. There are however a number of writers for the later period who make direct or implicit reference to military matters from which information on organisation and unit sizes may be gleaned.

Reference has already been made to the accusation by **Lactantius**[4] in his Christian polemic De Mortibus Persecutorum that Diocletian multiplied the existing army.[5] Although Lactantius was a contemporary of Diocletian and wrote his work only twenty years or so after the establishment of the Tetrarchy to which it refers, he had no personal military experience and it seems inherently more than improbable that this increase could actually have amounted to a quadrupling (if, in any case, that was what Lactantius was actually trying to write[6]). A doubling of the existing 33 legions seems to have taken place under Diocletian (although many would argue – as mentioned earlier – that these new legions at least were much smaller than the 5,000-strong ones of the Early Empire), and it has been suggested[7] that the imperial forces increased at the end of the third century by about a third from some 345,000 to perhaps 440,000 or so.

Writing towards the latter end of the fourth century was the distinguished academic **Libanius**. Libanius, a native of the Syrian Antioch, was an orator and professor of rhetoric in various cities of the Greek East. He referred incidentally to Diocletian as 'That emperor who set a wall of armed soldiery to defend the Roman empire ... .'[8] Writing of the same reign, Libanius recounted a story concerning a mutinous unit of 500 soldiers. The context of the anecdote makes the strength of the unit a marginal issue: he can possibly be assumed to be referring to a quingenary cohort but there is no real basis for confirming that assumption and the unit might equally well be a legionary vexillation or some sort of one-off working party.[9] Libanius himself had never seen military service.[10]

Roughly contemporary with Libanius, it is now generally agreed, were the so-called **Scriptores Historiae Augustae** (or 'Augustan History'). Although the work itself claims to have been written by six named authors in the reign of Diocletian, this appears to be entirely spurious: it seems to be the case that the work was actually written by a single, unknown author writing considerably later, probably in the 360s or 370s. The History's Life of Severus Alexander refers to that emperor's preparations for his Persian War in c. AD 230/231.[11] These preparations supposedly included the formation of a Greek-style phalanx of phalangarii 30,000-strong: the emperor is described as being obsessed with modelling himself on his namesake, Alexander the Great.

---

[1] See Chapter 2 page 21.
[2] Namely Legions I, V, VIII, IX, XIII, XIV, XV, XVI, XX and XXI (Tacitus, Annals, 1).
[3] Ibid., 1, 49 (26 cohorts and eight alae).
[4] See Chapter 2 page 14.
[5] Lactantius, 7, 2. The chapter contains other exaggerated jibes.
[6] Cf. John Casey, **The Legions in the Later Roman Empire: The Fourth Annual Caerleon Lecture**, Caerleon, 1991, page 12. Note the implication of Lactantius's use of the word 'contenderent.'
[7] By Casey, ibid., for example.
[8] Libanius, Orationes, 20, 17.
[9] Libanius, Orationes, 20, 18. The word used is 'pentakosion' = 'the 500'.
[10] This is perhaps however too often assumed to equate with complete ignorance of matters military. It could be remarked that – with some notable exceptions – most of the younger modern students of the Roman army have no first hand military experience either.
[11] SHA, Severus Alexander, 50, 5.

The alleged phalanx is interestingly described as '... formed from six legions.'[12] If this passage can be taken to imply that six **complete** legions were re-mustered as a phalanx, then the author appears to be calculating the individual legion strengths at 5,000 men. It is not necessary to see this little episode as other than probably entirely fictional nevertheless to allow the assertion that the author **believed** legions to be about 5,000 strong – at least in the 230s, if not in his own time.

Perhaps the most significant historian of the Late Empire and main source for the fourth century was **Ammianus Marcellinus** (c. AD 330 – c. 395). Ammianus was a soldier of substantial experience, serving probably until in his mid 30s or early 40s. Initially acting as a staff officer to the Master of the Horse, Ursicinus, Ammianus later saw active service in Gaul, Mesopotamia and on Julian's Persian expedition. He is generally well regarded as a source, being both fair and accurate, and was himself an eyewitness of some of the events he describes.

An impressively long list of regiments referred to by Ammianus can be compiled: Roger Tomlin has catalogued references to some four field army units and nearly thirty frontier regiments.[13] If we turn to army and unit sizes, Ammianus notes that Julian won his crowning victory over the Alamanni at Strasbourg in 357 when commanding only 13,000 men: in fact, he stresses that it was the smallness of Julian's army (of which news was carried by a deserter from the Scutarii) which helped to convince his enemies of his certain defeat.[14] It needs to be remembered however that this relatively small force under Julian was originally planned as half of a pincer movement against the Alamanni, the other part being a force of 25,000 under Barbatio, the Master of the Foot.[15] Although the junction of the two armies was not effected, a commitment of 38,000 troops was by no means insignificant: the army that invaded Britain in AD 43 was of that order.[16]

Ammianus was himself present at the siege of the cliff-top fortress city of Amida[17] when Shapur II invaded Mesopotamia in 359 and has left a detailed account of the battle.[18] Ammianus estimated the military and civilian population of Amida at 20,000[19] and also gives details of the garrison. Although he was writing from memory some thirty years later and although his description of the city is confused (or at least disoriented),[20] there is no reason to doubt the details of the units he lists. These, he wrote, included seven 'legions': the city's regular garrison unit, legio V Parthica; two legions raised under Magnentius and transferred from Gaul (Decentiaci and Magnentiaci); legiones XXX and X Fortenses; and the relatively new[21] Superventores and Praeventores.[22] There were evidently other units in the city too. Although the specified units all appear to have been Diocletianic or newer and there would therefore be no reason to assume 'old-style' 5,000-strong establishments, Ammianus's figures – if correct – would certainly imply much smaller legions. Jones suggested that Ammianus was therefore implying legions no more than about 1,000 men each[23] and this has become a widely accepted figure, although it amounts to little more than a reasonable probability. Jones himself added the qualification that some at least of the Amida garrison units may have been under-strength from campaign losses.

Ammianus includes a detailed account of a sally by the Gallic troops in Amida in which they suffered casualties of 400[24] but it is difficult to extrapolate much from that other than the reasonable assumption that the Gallic elements must therefore have numbered significantly in excess of 400.

If Ammianus is to be accepted as an accurate source for details of the siege of Amida, it might also be noted that he put the losses of the attacking Persians at 30,000.[25] This would make it difficult to envisage Shapur's besieging army as having an original strength of any less

---

[12] Ibid..
[13] Roger Tomlin, '**Seniores-Iuniores** in the Late-Roman Field Army', **American Journal of Philology** Vol. 93, 2, 1972, Appendix 1, pages 266-69.
[14] Ammianus Marcellinus, **Histories**, 16, 12, 2.
[15] Ibid., 16, 11, 2.
[16] Cf. Peter Salway, **Roman Britain**, The Oxford History of England 1A, Oxford, 1981, page 75.
[17] Modern Diyarbakir in south-east Turkey.
[18] Ammianus was only in his late 20s at the time of the siege, although his account of it was written probably in his late 50s or early 60s.
[19] It has been suggested (Roger Tomlin, **pers. comm.**) that a copying error might have resulted in a missing digit and that Ammianus actually wrote 120,000.
[20] He places Amida on the wrong bank of the Tigris, with Mesopotamia and the river Nymphaeus in the wrong direction.
[21] The **Superventores** and **Praeventores** had been raised a decade or so before.
[22] Ammianus, 18, 9, 3.
[23] A.H.M. Jones, **The Later Roman Empire 284-602: A Social, Economic and Administrative Survey**, Oxford, 1964, Volume 2, page 682.
[24] Ammianus, 19, 6, 11.
[25] Ammianus, 19, 9, 9.

than 40,000 men; 60,000 or 70,000 or even more would not seem unreasonable to have sustained such losses. If the Roman army in Amida is to be reckoned at a strength of no more than some 10,000, then it is most impressive that it inflicted such casualties on the Persians and withstood a siege of over ten weeks, especially as it can be argued that the fall of the city was caused only by an unfortunate combination of treachery and bad luck. The Persian casualties and the long delay at Amida were in any case sufficient to persuade Shapur to abandon the campaign and return to Ctesiphon. The strength of the city's defences may have played a rôle in the 74-day siege but Amida's renowned black basalt walls date essentially from a later period.[26]

It might be possible to hesitate before accepting easily Ammianus's figure for the Persian dead: enemy casualties are a notoriously difficult area for estimation, arguably even in modern circumstances.[27] Ammianus does however go out of his way to cite his sources, even naming the officer who seems to have been assigned to count the dead.[28] Ammianus is in any case impressively well informed about Shapur's army, for which he is even able to provide an outline order of battle.[29]

Although Ammianus himself took part in Julian's great Persian campaign of 363 and describes the war at length, he provides little of the detail of numbers and units that would be of use to the current purpose. Julian's army is elsewhere put at 65,000 men[30] and this would not be inconsistent with the statement by Ammianus that 30,000 troops under Count Procopius were detached to Armenia to guard the rear of Julian's advance.[31] The only other statistic in Ammianus's account is the reference to the 20,000 troops that had been needed to tow and manoeuvre the thousand ships that had accompanied the advance down the Euphrates.[32] Of the scores of units that must have formed Julian's expedition, Ammianus names barely half a dozen. The field army Victores regiment is mentioned at the siege of Maozamalcha: a soldier from the unit called Exsuperius led the assault from a mine the engineers had dug.[33] A cavalry formation identified only as Tertiaci are described as disgracing themselves during a Persian attack and then apparently being disbanded.[34] The comitatensian legion Zianni is mentioned because its commander, Vetranio, was killed driving off a Persian attack.[35] Then, following Julian's death on 26th June and the accession of Jovian, four other field army units are mentioned as distinguishing themselves during a Persian attack with elephants on the rearguard: the Ioviani and the Herculiani (legiones palatinae), and the Iovii and the Victores (auxilia palatina).[36] The Antioch-based lawyer, Ioannes (John) Malalas included some further details of this campaign in his Greek world chronicle, composed probably in the 560s or 570s. He notes a unit of 1,500 lanciarii and mattiarii, and the legion I Armenaica as forming part of Julian's army.[37]

Two of Ammianus's references to events in Britain detail the composition of field army expeditions sent to the island under Lupicinus in AD 360 and Theodosius in 367-8.[38] Only four units were involved on each occasion: in 360 the Heruli and Batavi (described as 'lightly armed'[39]) together with two numeri of Moesians; and in 367 Heruli and Batavi again, this time accompanied by Iovii and Victores. It might reasonably be asked how such limited military intervention could have been expected to be of any significance. However these expeditionary forces may have been up to about 3,000 strong[40] and this is perhaps not such a small figure in the context of estimates for the strength of the fourth century British garrison, which have ranged down to as few as 12,000 men. In any case both expeditions in the 360s seem to have had fairly limited 'spearhead' rôles: it has been said that '... their main

---

[26] Although they may already have been anticipated in a more basic form (Roger Tomlin, **pers. comm.**).
[27] Cf. for example the wide variations in estimates of casualties suffered by the Iraqi forces in the 1991 Gulf War.
[28] Diascenes (Ammianus, 19, 9, 9).
[29] Ibid., 18, 6, 22. Ammianus lists the Chionitae (under their king Grumbates), the Cuseni (Kushans), the Albani and the Segestani (the latter accompanied by a force of elephants, about which he seems particularly anxious).
[30] Zosimus, **Nea Historia**, 3,13, 1. This can be read as referring only to the strength of the main force less the Tigris detachment (implying a full strength of 83,000 men).
[31] Ammianus, 23, 3, 5. (16,000 according to Malalas 13, 21, and 18,000 according to Zosimus [op. cit., 3, 12, 4]).
[32] Ammianus, 24, 7, 4.
[33] Ibid., 24, 4, 23.
[34] Ibid., 25, 1, 7.
[35] Ibid., 25, 1, 19.
[36] Ibid., 25, 6, 2-3.
[37] John Malalas, 13, 21 and 13, 23.
[38] Ammianus, 20, 1, 3 and 27, 8, 7.
[39] Ibid., 20, 1, 3. The expression 'velitari' might mean something like 'light infantry' but might equally suggest that in this emergency the troops were deployed unencumbered, for example, by baggage.
[40] Personal comment from Roger Tomlin, referring for example to Hoffmann's estimates.

purpose could have only been to raise local morale.'[41] We have in fact no clear indication from Ammianus of any campaigning involving Lupicinus's force, and Theodosius's four regiments seem only to have been used on their own against bands of looters.[42] The major counter-attacks against the barbarian invaders were undertaken by a force apparently formed largely from returning deserters and troops on leave from the original garrison. It should also be noted that, in the case of the first of these expeditions at least, whatever measures were undertaken by the field army detachments, they were no more than short-term in effect (and perhaps even in intention): Ammianus himself recorded just four years after Lupicinus's visit to Britain attacks by Picts, Scots, Saxons and Attacotti 'aerumnis ... continuis.'[43]

The disastrous battle at Adrianople (9 August 378) forms the climax of Ammianus's history but his account is disappointingly lacking in organisational details. He himself had earlier referred to the difficulties of estimating the numbers of Goths, as he had when declining to catalogue Shapur's Persian army.[44] He does conclude his account of the battle with a reference to casualties but this does no more than list the distinguished dead and claim that about two-thirds of Valens's army were lost in the disaster.

Modern accounts have put the Roman army at Adrianople as low as c. 15-18,000 or as high as 30-40,000 while Hoffmann has used the Notitia to identify some of the mobile army units lost there. Ammianus himself however refers to a mere handful of regiments. He mentions the Sagitarii and Scutarii who seem to have launched the opening assault of the battle; the Lanciarii and Mattiarii, who protected Valens after his own bodyguard had fled; the Batavi, who failed to act in their assigned reserve rôle; and the Stablesiani, Domestici and Promoti – units whose commanders fell in the battle.

Elsewhere in his history, however, are a scatter of other references by Ammianus to unit sizes and organisation. In his account of his own arrival at Amida in the spring of 359,

Ammianus tells the story of two units (the word he uses unfortunately is 'turmae') of cavalry sent from Illyricum ('a feeble and cowardly lot') who, while in 'drunken sleep', allowed a force of 20,000 Persians to slip by at night unseen. Ammianus specifically mentions that these two units of Danubian cavalry had a total strength of 700.[45] The implicit individual unit strength of about 350 might reasonably be seen as representing a theoretical establishment of around 500 in campaigning circumstances.

In his account of Julian being hailed Augustus in 360, Ammianus mentions a rather odd incident when Constantius, allegedly jealous of Julian's successes in the West, ordered to be detached from his army for campaigning against the Persians four of his best auxiliary regiments (Heruli, Batavi, Celts and Petulantes) together with 300 picked men from each of the other units under his command ('ex numeris aliis trecentos').[46] This can be seen as a remarkable snub, especially bearing in mind the relatively small size of Julian's army, but the important point is that Constantius's order would only have made sense if the units in question had been substantially larger than, say, 500 strong each. It may be in fact that what is being witnessed here is the standard process for creating detachments or sub-dividing units – although here used to weaken Julian's position.

When recording the restoration to the throne of Hiberia (the kingdom east of Armenia in the area of Georgia) in AD 370 of King Sauromaces, Ammianus states that he was accompanied by '12 legions' under the general Terentius.[47] This would certainly be an impressive force, even if the reference were to relatively small Late Army legions but, for a military man, Ammianus is remarkably imprecise in his use of terminology and he may well have meant 12 auxilia or simply something vaguer along the lines of '12 units.'

Finally, in his narrative of events leading up to Adrianople in 378, Ammianus includes a couple of interesting asides about field army unit sizes. Gratian is said to have picked 500 veterans

---

[41] N.J.E. Austin, **Ammianus on Warfare: An Investigation into Ammianus' Military Knowledge**, Collection Latomus Volume 165, Brussels, 1979, page 109.
[42] Ammianus, 27, 8, 7: '... roving parties of freebooters' in the Penguin translation (Walter Hamilton and Andrew Wallace-Hadrill, Harmondsworth, 1986, page 343).
[43] Ibid., 26, 4, 5.
[44] Ibid., 31, 5, 10 and 18, 6, 23.

[45] Ibid., 18, 8, 2.
[46] Ibid., 20, 4, 2. Zosimus (3, 8, 4) describes how, after already having demanded two 'Celtic legions [*tagmata*]', Constantius ordered more legions to be detached from Julian's army, followed by four cavalry 'regiments [*tagmata*]'. Libanius (**Orationes** 18, 94) refers to the incident without giving details, while Julian himself (**Letter to the Athenians** 280D) says he sent four, then another three, *arithmoi* of infantry and two *tagmata* of cavalry.
[47] Ibid., 27, 12, 16.

from each of his legions to scale the heights held by the Alamannic Lentienses.[48] Shortly afterwards, we hear of the Master of Infantry, Count Sebastian, being assigned a force made up of 300 soldiers detached from each of his units ('numeri') to use in counter-guerrilla warfare against the Goths in Thrace. It needs only be stressed that these references need to assume actual unit strengths substantially larger than the detachments detailed: say, 500–1,000 strong.[49]

A near contemporary of Ammianus was the court poet **Claudian** (Claudius Claudianus), an Egyptian who lived between c. AD 370 and c. 404. In 397 the Mauretanian chieftain and former Count of Africa, Gildo, rose in revolt against Stilicho and the government in Milan. Fearing especially the threat to the supply of grain from Africa to Italy, Stilicho despatched an expedition against Gildo the next spring commanded by his own estranged brother, Mascezel. Claudian later composed the poem In Gildonem in praise of Stilicho's rôle in the war. Included in this panegyric is what amounts to an order of battle for Mascezel's army: it apparently comprised the Herculiani and Ioviani seniores (both described as 'cohorts'); the Nervii; the Felices iuniores; the 'legion' Augusti (VIII Augusta?); and the Leones iuniores.[50] This seems too circumstantial a detail to be fictional and, apart from the vague Augusti, the other five units are all recorded in the Notitia as field army infantry regiments – four of them stationed in Italy.[51] By a useful coincidence, the early fifth century Christian historian **Orosius** (Paulus Orosius) also referred to the expedition against Gildo in his defence of Christianity, Historia Adversus Paganos, written some 19 years after the event. Orosius put the strength of Mascezel's task force at about 5,000 men and this has been used, for example, by Várady,[52] as a means of attempting to calculate the size of the field army units in the campaign of 398. A simple calculation (assuming the 6 regiments were of roughly the same size) would produce an average figure of rather more than 800 men.[53] This would fit in quite well with the range of 500–1,000 suggested by some scholars as being likely for fourth century mobile army units.[54] Várady however suggests a more complicated solution: he puts the three palatine legions (the first three units detailed above) at 1,200 each (a total of 3,600), while calculating the three 'auxiliary' formations at only 500 each.[55]

Living at very much the same time as Claudian was the philosopher and writer, **Synesius** of Cyrene (c. AD 370 – c. 412/415), bishop of Ptolemais in Egypt from c. AD 410/411. As well as 156 letters, Synesius wrote hymns, a political allegory and a treatise On Kingship. As a prominent landowner, Synesius had also played a rôle in leading armed resistance to raids by the desert barbarians. Cyrenaica was under threat from the nomadic or semi-nomadic Macetae and Ausurians from southern Numidia and Tripolitania, made more dangerous by their use of camels. Between AD 404 and 411 the Cyrenaican countryside was regularly overrun by these tribes, and a more serious invasion occurred in 412. Regular Roman troops seem to have been dispersed in forts and particularly the cities, and to have put up a poor defence. Synesius's writings however make several references to Imperial forces called Unnigardae: these appear to have been Hunnish federate cavalrymen.

At one point, for example, Synesius states that in 411 forty Unnigardae were 'with us' and another 200 with his associate, Anysius.[56] In a letter to the same Anysius,[57] Synesius recounts the apparently dramatic defeat of a force of rather more than 1,000 Ausurian barbarians, who were ambushed in a narrow defile by his small force of forty Unnigardae. It may be that this account can be accepted at face value and that the factors of topography referred to by Synesius do help to explain a victory which, although remarkable, was far from

---

[48] Ibid., 31, 10, 13.
[49] Cf., for example, Roger Tomlin, 'The Late-Roman Empire' in General Sir John Hackett (ed.), **Warfare in the Ancient World**, London, 1989, page 238. Is the relative frequency of references to detachments of 300 troops coincidence or is it evidence of some kind of norm?
[50] Claudian, **In Gildonem**, 418-423.
[51] Namely, *Herculiani seniores* (**N.D.** Oc. 5, 146 and 7, 4, Italy), *Ioviani seniores* (**N.D.** Oc. 5, 145 and 7, 3, Italy), *Nervii* (**N.D.** Or. 5, 46, the East), *Felices iuniores* (**N.D.** Oc. 5, 180 and 7, 23, Italy) and *Leones iuniores* (**N.D.** Oc. 5, 172 and 7, 19, Italy).
[52] L. Várady, 'New Evidences on Some Problems of the Late Roman Military Organisation', **Acta Antiqua Academiae Scientiarum Hungaricae** Tomus 9, Budapest, 1961, pages 333–96, quoting Orosius, **Historia contra paganos**, 7, 36, 6.
[53] $5,000 \div 6 = 833$.
[54] Cf. note 49 above.
[55] Várady, op. cit. (note 52). Várady's calculations give the force an exact size of 5,100: $3 \times 1,200 + 3 \times 500 = 5,100$.
[56] Synesius, **Constitutio**, 1576.
[57] Synesius, **Letter 78**. In **Letter** 125 Synesius is clearly referring to irregulars enrolled at his own expense, and it seems at least possible that none of his exploits involved regular troops and that any statistics cited are irrelevant when considering **unit** sizes.

unprecedented when Imperial forces were pitted against poorly equipped and untrained barbarians.[58] It is in any case not easy to extrapolate from this anecdote an assumption that Late Roman mobile cavalry formations typically numbered fewer than fifty troopers. Synesius himself goes on to suggest that another 160 Unnigardae would be sufficient to finish this campaign and it seems considerably easier to take this as a reference to additional federate troops rather than as any sort of precise reference to, for example, an extra four cavalry regiments.[59] It is perhaps a reflection of the scale of the fighting involved in Cyrenaica that Synesius felt that the more critical invasion the next year (412) could be defeated by four centuries of infantry.[60]

Vegetius (Flavius Vegetius Renatus) wrote a number of works between c. AD 383 and c. 450: possibly a Spaniard, it has been suggested that he may have been a finance minister or comes sacri stabuli of Theodosius I. At some date probably between 383 and 392 Vegetius wrote his Epitoma Rei Militaris or De Re Militari, in which he described the weakness of Roman infantry and suggested strategies for improvement. Vegetius has not been held in high esteem in modern times, being criticised as an amateur on military matters with a nostalgic longing for a return of the classic legions. He was however held in remarkably high regard in mediaeval and early modern Europe: 150 mediaeval manuscripts of his work, for example, survive.

Vegetius has already been referred to[61] as one of the authorities for placing the size of a turma at 32 men and this still seems on balance the most likely figure, although it is usually argued that he was referring back to a period not later than the end of the third century rather than to his own days. It is interesting to note that Vegetius – who did after all live through the supposed triumph of cavalry over heavy infantry at Adrianople – has little concern with the qualities of Roman cavalry forces: '... cum praesens doctrina sufficiat.'[62]

Vegetius's work included an intriguing reference to two legions 6,000 men strong which had 'formerly' defended the Illyrian frontier over a long period with their mattiobarbuli or lead-weighted darts; they were later honoured with the titles Jovian and Herculean by Diocletian and Maximian.[63] It is not entirely clear what Vegetius was trying to write here and it has been argued that the period at which the legions had the classical strength of 6,000 could have been substantially pre-Diocletianic.[64] It is also quite possible to consider these two legions to have been entirely fictional but, if Vegetius's statement is taken at something like face value, there would appear to have been legionary units in Illyricum at the accession of Diocletian and Maximian (AD 286) with the traditional 6,000-strong establishment. Even if this figure is accepted as accurate, it does not of course have any implications either for legions outside Illyricum or for those of periods later than the late third century. On the other hand, there is at least the possibility of legions at traditional strength in one area of the Empire only some 14 years before documentary evidence from another area has been interpreted as recording legions nearly six times smaller. It may well be that, as well as accepting the possibility that there may have been two different legionary establishments (for those raised before and after the 280s), there may also have been different actual strengths due to factors such as battle casualties or slack recruiting during periods of inactivity.

Finally Vegetius includes an interesting comment on fort sizes: '... the size of the camp should be proportional to the number of troops. A camp which is too confined will not permit the troops to perform their movements with freedom, and one which is too extensive divides them too much.' ('Nam propugnatores angusta constipant et ultra quam convenit latiora diffundunt.')[65] Even from a military amateur, this seems unexceptionable common sense and should perhaps be borne in mind when considering suggestions for drastically reduced

---

[58] At Strasbourg in 357, for example, Julian defeated 32,000 Germans with an army of just 13,000. Ammianus (16, 12, 63) puts Roman casualties at 247 dead while the enemy lost at least 6,000.
[59] The Loeb translator of Synesius (Augustine Fitzgerald, 1926) suspects exaggeration in this letter and makes an interesting comparison with the account by Sidonius Apollinaris (**Letters** 3, 3, 3–4) of his brother-in-law Ecdidius defeating a force of several thousand Goths with only 18 men! Gregory of Tours later reduced even this minuscule force to just ten (**Hist. Franc**. 2, 24). This incident took place in AD 474, just fifty years after Synesius's death. It has recently been suggested however [Whittaker 1993 page 295] that 'we are here victims of terminology' and that the small figures cited are references to Ecdidius's *satellites* and not his whole army.
[60] Synesius, **Constitutio**, 1576 and 1563.
[61] See Chapter 1 page 2.

[62] Vegetius, 3, 26.
[63] Ibid., 1, 17. Vegetius states that each soldier carried five 'darts' in his shield.
[64] John Casey, op. cit. (note 6), page 13.
[65] Vegetius, 3, 8.

garrison numbers – resulting, for example, in a two-hectare [five-acre] fort held by just over eighty soldiers.[66]

Zosimus was a Greek-speaking pagan from the East, possibly a native of Constantinople – a city he knew well. At some time between c. AD 450 and c. 503 – probably later rather than earlier – he compiled his New History, a sort of digest of the work of earlier historians, especially Eunapius and Olympiodorus of Thebes. The work contains a number of incidental references to unit and army sizes. He calculates, for example, a Western army of some 286,000 in 312: 98,000 under Constantine and 188,000 under Maxentius.[67] There is nothing particularly incredible in this figure; nor is there in Zosimus's estimate that Julian's Persian expedition of 363 numbered 65,000 men.[68] The latter has become widely accepted and is perfectly acceptable: it is a reasonably modest size compared with some ancient army estimates, although it may have been the largest Imperial expedition ever put into the field.

Early in the next century, the invasion of Italy by the Ostrogoth leader Radagaisus (AD 405) was halted, Zosimus claimed, by a surprise attack from an army led by Stilicho: this force apparently comprised some Alan and Hunnish irregulars together with thirty regular mobile army units.[69] It seems difficult to envisage this force at anything much larger than 30,000 men, which makes the total rout of 400,000 'Celts and Germans' less than easy to credit. It is worth noting therefore that Orosius estimated the barbarian force at only 200,000 or slightly more,[70] while Augustine reckoned it at more than 100,000 but including many non-combatants.[71] In other ways too, Zosimus's account of the events of 405 seems unsatisfactory. The army of Radagaisus may perhaps have included Vandals and Silings as well as Goths but reference to Celts make little sense. Furthermore, there seems not to have been a bloody battle as described by Zosimus but rather the blockade of a hill ('de Fiesole' or 'Faesulae') followed by a capitulation. There were apparently very few deaths: in fact, Orosius wrote that so many prisoners were taken that the price of a slave fell to one gold piece. Olympiodorus also contradicts Zosimus's claim that a 'few' of the defeated barbarians were enrolled as auxiliaries: he refers to no fewer than 12,000 high-born conscripts.

An implicit reference to unit sizes occurs when Zosimus records that Honorius, concerned that Rome was 'in no better position than before,' ordered to the city from their Dalmatian bases five legions comprising '6,000 men in all'[72] in January or February 409. Although the phrase used by Zosimus means 'formations [tagmata] of troops', this does seem to be a reference to field army legions well over 1,000 strong.[73] Zosimus incidentally goes on to recount that the five 'legions' were ambushed en route to Rome by Alaric and all but 100 were taken prisoner.

The next year, according to Zosimus, six long expected units arrived in Ravenna from the East: '... they numbered 4,000.'[74] This could be interpreted as a reference to cohorts some 600–700 strong: the Greek word used is tagmata.[75] It should be noted that, although there are exceptions, many Greek-speaking writers clearly found transliterating Latin technical terms aesthetically undesirable and preferred to seek classical analogies: these were often quite inappropriate, such as 'phalanx'.[76]

Eugippius (c. AD 460–533+) was the abbot of a monastery near Naples, who was possibly a native of Noricum. He is well known for his Vita Severini, a life of Saint Severinus, an Easterner who lived between c. AD 455 and 8 January 482, and visited Noricum probably in the 460s. This biography has become a popular source in recent times for the state of the Late Army and also as providing an analogy for the less well recorded decline of the military establishment in early fifth century Britain.[77] What Eugippius recorded in the Vita was presumably the remnant of the very large garrisons of the same region recorded in the Notitia (Oc. 34 and 35): these totalled two cunei, 17 units of equites, eight legionary detachments (from four different legions), a group of Marcomanni, three alae, 11 cohorts, a

---

[66] Namely, Housesteads: see Chapter 5 page 53.
[67] Zosimus, 2, 15, 1-2. The **Panegyric** of Constantine puts Maxentius's troops at 100,000 (9, 3, 3) and Constantine's at under 40,000 (9, 5, 1-2).
[68] Ibid., 3, 12-13. But see note 30 above.
[69] Ibid., 5, 26, 4. This is a particularly circumstantial account, which has at least a superficial air of credibility. The word used for 'unit' is 'arithmos', the usual Greek equivalent for 'numerus'.
[70] Orosius, op. cit. (note 52), 7, 39, 4, 13.
[71] Augustine, **City of God**, 5, 23.

[72] Zosimus, 5, 45, 1.
[73] 1,200 if Zosimus was using figures precisely.
[74] Ibid., 6, 8, 2. The manuscript actually reads 40,000. Sozomen (9, 8, 6) confirms 4,000.
[75] 666 would be an exact calculation.
[76] Cf. John Lydus, **On Powers**, Part 2, 6, 5.
[77] Cf. for example, David J. Breeze and Brian Dobson, **Hadrian's Wall**, London, 1976, page 231.

detachment of Raetians and four river patrol forces. Even allowing the smallest possible establishments for these units, it has to be concluded that the Notitia was recording (probably in the late fourth century – perhaps only eighty years or so before the visit of Severinus) several thousand troops at least defending this crucial section of the upper Danube. Severinus however appeared to have encountered just a couple of surviving units in the 460s. At Favianis (the modern Mautern in Austria) Eugippius recorded that Severinus found a small contingent (milites paucissimi) under a tribune; this base had earlier (according to the Notitia) housed a riverine detachment of the legion I Noricorum.[78] At the modern Passau in Bavaria Severinus apparently found a small garrison, which is usually taken to be the final remnant of cohors IX Batavorum (a unit which had been at Passau so long that it had given its name to the fort[79]). It is not unreasonable to assume that Eugippius's silence in regards to the other garrisons implies that most, if not all, of them had been abandoned. Eugippius records the fall of one of these, Ioviacum (modern Schlögen in Austria, base of a 'naval' detachment of legio II Italica according to the Notitia[80]), to the Heruli in a single night at some point in or after 472.

Eugippius also describes the fall of Favianis to the Rugi under their king Feletheus or Feva and (in c. AD 476) of Passau/Batavis. He had earlier recorded the famous incident when the Passau troops, finding their pay had not arrived, sent a delegation to Italy seeking redress;[81] the bodies of these soldiers were later found floating in the Inn. When the barbarians under Hunumundus finally captured Passau, the forty survivors were all killed:[82] it is obviously open to question as to what this should be taken to imply about the final strength of the Ninth Batavians other than it must presumably have been rather larger than forty, although not necessarily very much more.

It should finally be noted that, although Eugippius does record that the Norican towns continued to hold out beyond the fall of the remaining military posts, he nowhere makes reference to the Danube fleet which must once have been a substantial force.

Ioannes Lydus (or John the Lydian) was born at Philadelphia in Lydia in c. AD 490 and lived until towards the end of Justinian's reign (that is, before 565). After a career in the civil administration in Constantinople, Lydus became an academic and was perhaps the most distinguished antiquarian of his period; he was noted for his knowledge of Latin – by then a rarity in the East. His writings included works of panegyric, history and poetry. In the current context, it is worth noting that, although he had experience of matters of government, scholarship and the law, he had none of military affairs.

Towards the end of his life (between AD 554 and 565), Lydus wrote a work usually known as De Magistratibus or On Powers, a sort of study of Roman institutions. In this book Lydus describes, purporting to refer to the war against the Veii in 388 BC, the establishment of units of particular sizes.[83] These units included cohorts of 500 'shield-bearers,' alae of 600, vexillations of 500 horsemen, turmae [sic] of 500 horse archers, and legions of 6,000 infantry. It is not easy to make much sense of this passage. It does not seem to refer with much accuracy to real Republican units of this very early period but nor does it seem that Lydus is anachronistically describing Imperial forces of his own period. As well as his terminology, Lydus's chronology seems suspect.[84]

Before dimissing Lydus's figures as a complete nonsense however, it should be noted that some individual elements – such as the 6,000-strong legion – are perfectly feasible ones for the early Empire or even the Republic. Furthermore, Lydus elsewhere[85] cites figures for Diocletian's army which do not seem ridiculous. He put the army at 389,704 men (plus 45,562 in the fleet, for a grand total of 435,266), which would fit quite well with other estimates for the situation at Diocletian's accession at least[86] and should cause some hesitation before judging his statements to be entirely without value.

A near contemporary of Lydus was the poet and lawyer, **Agathias** (c. AD 532 – c. 579/582), who wrote in the late 560s an Historia, of which the first five books survive covering the

---

[78] N.D. Oc. 34, 41.
[79] Ibid., Oc. 35, 24. Cohors IX Batavorum had been at Passau since c. AD 166 – that is, about 310 years when the fort fell.
[80] Ibid., Oc. 34, 37.
[81] Eugippius, Vita Severini, 20, 1.
[82] Ibid., 22, 4.

[83] John Lydus, On Powers, Part 1, Chapter 46.
[84] He refers to 365 AUC (= 389 BC) but seems to cite the consuls for 389 AUC (= 365 BC). Veii had been captured by 396 BC (cf. Livy Book 5). It has been pointed out (John Matthews, pers. comm.) that many modern scholars are less than well versed in the use of modern military organisational terminology!
[85] John Lydus De Mensibus, 1, 27.
[86] Cf. Chapter 2 page 14.

years 552–559. Describing a serious invasion of the Hunnish Cottigurs under Zabergan in 559, Agathias records that they reached the walls of Constantinople unmolested. In a bitter passage, he attributes the barbarians' success to the 'drastic reductions in the armed forces incurred through the negligence of the authorities' who had allowed the Roman army to dwindle from an establishment of 645,000 men to 'barely 150,000' including units stationed in Italy, Spain, Lazica in the Caucasus, Egypt and on the Persian border.[87] These figures – especially the latter – are not intrinsically unbelievable, even if they are taken only to reflect the strength of the mobile armies excluding the limitanei.

Another sixth century Byzantine writer, **Procopius,** gives no figures for unit sizes but does include some interesting references to the total numbers in certain expeditionary forces. The army that Anastasius led against the Persians in 503, for example, Procopius estimated at 52,000 men;[88] he said that Belisarius commanded 25,000 troops on the Eastern front in 530 and 20,000 the next year.[89] Referring to such sixth century armies, ranging in size from some 8,000 to over 50,000 men, Jones wisely reminded us that: 'These small figures need not, however, throw doubts on the gross totals. With all large armies it is difficult to put into the field for a given campaign more than a very small proportion of their total numbers; the great majority of the troops are tied down by local commitments. This was markedly the case with the later Roman empire. The limitanei in the first place were committed to local defence and internal security duties: ... they were not available for a major campaign. They accounted ... for about two-thirds of the total at the end of the fourth century.'[90]

It could indeed be argued that, even by modern standards, the figures cited by ancient authorities are high rather than otherwise: the 65,000 men that Julian is usually agreed to have led into Persia in 363 must have represented at least 10% or 15% of the entire Imperial army, mobile or not. This compares, for example, with the 12.75% of total armed forces comprising the peak US deployment to Vietnam in 1969 or the UK's deployment of 8.5% of its forces to the Falklands in 1982; neither of these powers of course also had a frontier defence task of quite the nature that faced Julian.

Procopius, incidentally, refers to the presence of a 'legion' at Melitene [V Macedonica] in a manner which implies his unfamiliarity with the term – or at least his assumption that his readers would be unfamiliar with the word. At the time he was writing legions evidently continued to form part of the Imperial forces, as the reference by Theophylact Simocatta to IV Parthica indicates.[91]

Table 3 below is a schematic method of representing the unit size references contained in this chapter. The picture it summarises is far from consistent or clear. It seems to provide evidence both for units much smaller than the assumed establishments of the Principate (Ammianus and Synesius, for example) and for apparent survivals of traditionally sized formations (recorded, for instance, by Libanius and Vegetius). There are therefore no simple conclusions. It may be that an image of inconsistency is best explained as representing a reality of inconsistency. It may be however that our evidence is too limited and too random to allow any lessons to be learnt. And it may be of course that writers of literature, often with little or no military experience, should always be considered with caution.

---

[87] Agathias, **The Histories**, Book 5, 13, 6–8. Agathias goes on to describe how the aged Belisarius was persuaded from retirement and defeated the Huns with just 300 veterans and a rabble of unarmed Constantinopolitans and peasants. He claims that 400 Huns were killed but no Romans.
[88] Procopius, **De Bello Persico**, 1, 8, 4.
[89] Ibid..
[90] Jones, op. cit. (note 23), Volume 2, page 685.

[91] Procopius, **Buildings**, 3, 4, 16. Cf. Chapter 2, note 9.

Table 3: 4th/6th Century Literary References to Unit Sizes

Author	Date	Date Referred to	Unit Sizes
Libanius	Late 4th C	Diocletianic	Cohorts (?) of 500
SHA	360s/70s+	c. 230/1	Legions of 5,000
Vegetius	383/392	Pre-Diocletianic (?)	Legions of 6,000
Ammianus	Early 390s	354	7 legions totalling well under 20,000 2 cavalry 'turmae' totalling 700
Claudian	Early 5th C	398	Field army units of about 800
Synesius	Early 5th C	411	Cavalry unit (?) of 40
Zosimus	Late 5th C	409	Legions (?) of about 1,200 Cohorts (?) of about 666
Eugippius	Early 6th C?	c. 476	Cohort of 40+?
John Lydus	554/565	380s BC?	Cohorts of 300 Alae of 600 Cavalry vexillations of 500
John Malalas	574+	363	Turmae of 500 Legions of 6,000 Unit of 1,500 lanciarii and mattiarii

CHAPTER 4
LATER DOCUMENTARY EVIDENCE

This chapter will consider the evidence provided by the two major documentary sources which actually date from the fourth century. Although neither of these sources provides <u>direct</u> evidence for unit sizes, both have been widely used for this purpose and their implications have become central to discussion of the issue.

A: The Panopolis Papyri

These papyri, published in Dublin in 1964, comprise two fragments from the files of the Strategus (or sub-Governor) of the Panopolite nome at Panopolis in Upper Egypt, recording <u>inter alia</u> communications with 11 units of the provincial garrison: (1) copies of letters sent by him in September 298 and (2) letters received by him shortly afterwards from the Procurator (or Governor) of the Lower Thebaid.[1] (The Lower Thebaid was the area administered from Thebes, the southernmost of the three main districts of Roman Egypt, which seems to have been a province newly created by the time of these papyri. It was governed by an <u>epitropos</u> or Procurator, and was in turn sub-divided into nine of the traditional Egyptian districts called nomes, each controlled by a strategus.)

Panopolis 1 includes copies of two letters dated 24 September 298. The first (lines 392-394) orders the 'overseers of barley' to supply the soldiers at the fort of Thmoö under the Prefect Papas with 2,610 Italic modii for the two months 29 August to 27 October 298.[2] The second letter (lines 395-398) has the same date and orders the Decemprimi of the Middle Toparchy to supply the same garrison for the same two months with 1287/8 artabas of wheat from the produce of the year 296/7. We know from later in the papyri that the garrison unit at Thmoö was the cavalry regiment ala I Hiberorum. The <u>Notitia</u> also records the same situation with the regiment being one of the 16 alae in the very large command of the dux Thebaidos.[3]

Panopolis Papyrus 2 comprises a large file of 16 letters received at Panopolis as detailed below:
1) An order (lines 27-31) dated 4 February 300 from Aurelius Isidorus, Procurator of the Lower Thebaid, to Apolinarius, the <u>strategos</u> of the Panopolite <u>nome</u> to recover 21,000 denarii from seven soldiers[4] of the ala II Herculia Dromedariorum commanded by the Prefect Eudaemon. Later in the papyrus this camel unit is placed at the joint forts of Toëto and Psinabla; the <u>Notitia</u> also records the regiment at the latter place (called there Psinaula).[5] This money (3,000 denarii per man) does not appear to be a simple over-issue of pay but it is far from clear what else it might be.
2) An order (lines 36-42) dated 9 February 300 (sent on 30 January) from the Procurator to the same <u>strategos</u> and the Panopolite 'receivers' to pay 73,500 denarii in <u>stipendium</u> for 1 January 300 to the troops of ala I Hiberorum (or Iberorum) at Thmoö under the decurion Besas.[6] Although nowhere stated to be so, this payment is usually assumed to represent a 4-month instalment with the other thirds paid on 1 May and 1 September; the annual <u>stipendium</u> bill for the unit would therefore have totalled 220,500 denarii. The unit is also ordered to be paid for the four month period 1 September to 31 December 299 as <u>annona</u> (here presumably a cash substitute for provision in kind) 23,600 denarii.
3) A letter (lines 57-60) sent on 30 January 300 and received on 11 February from the Procurator to the <u>strategos</u> and 'receivers' ordering them to pay 343,300 denarii as <u>stipendium</u> for 1 January 300 to the legionaries of the legion III Diocletiana serving in the headquarters of the Governor ('Praeses') of the whole Thebaid, Julius Athenodorus. The payment is ordered to be made to the leading centurion, Dioscorus, presumably this vexillation's <u>praepositus</u>.

---

[1] T.C. Skeat (ed.), **Papyri from Panopolis: In The Chester Beatty Library Dublin**, Chester Beatty Monographs No. 10, Dublin, 1964.
[2] The item to be supplied is nowhere explicitly stated but can safely be ssumed to have been barley for horse fodder.
[3] **Notitia Dignitatum**, Or. 31, 46. The station for the unit is also spelt Thmu and Thmuis; suggested modern equivalents include (Tel-e-) Tmai and Essawieh el-Charq. The latter is on the right bank of the Nile four miles upriver of Panopolis. An Oxyrhynchus papyrus (**P.Oxy.** 2953) also confirms the ala as being at this base.
[4] Five of the soldiers' names survive in the papyrus: Ammonius (a cataphract), Peteësis (a decurion), Serapion (summus curator?), Isidorus (an actuarius) and another Ammonius.
[5] **P. Beatty Panop.** 2, line 169; **Notitia Dignitatum**, Or. 31, 54.
[6] Note that the unit has a new, presumably temporary, commander: more than 16 months had passed since Papas was recorded as its prefect. The reference to Besas as commander might however imply that only a detachment of the ala was stationed at Thmoö (cf. M.A. Speidel 1992, page 99).

4) A letter (lines 161–167) sent on 8 February 300 and received 11 days later in which the Procurator orders the strategos and receivers to pay 302,500[7] denarii to the horse archers[8] under the praepositus Valerius at Potecoptus[9] to celebrate the anniversary of the accession of Diocletian (20 November 284) and an identical amount to celebrate the emperor's birthday (22 December).

5) A letter (lines 168–175) sent with the previous one in which the Procurator orders two donatives for the same occasions of 53,750 denarii each to be paid to the soldiers of ala II Herculia Dromedariorum at Toëto and Psinabla under the Prefect Eudaemon.

6) A letter (lines 180–185) sent on 31 January 300 and received on 26 February ordering payment of 1,386,250 denarii to the soldiers of the vexillation of legio II Traiana at Apollinopolis Superior[10] under the praepositus Leontius; this sum was to be paid as donatives for the emperor's birthday.

7) One of four letters (lines 186–190) sent on 18 February 300 and received eight days later in which the Procurator orders an accession donative of 2,496,250 denarii to be paid to the troops of a vexillation made up from 'various Eastern legions' at Potecoptus under the praepositus Mucianus.[11]

8) A similar letter to seven above (lines 192–196) ordering a birthday donative of an identical amount.

9) One of two letters (lines 197–203) sent on 26 February 300 and received the next day (!) in which the Procurator orders payment of two sums of 2,500 denarii each to Leontius, praepositus of the equites promoti of the legion II Traiana at Tentyra[12] as arrears of donatives and 18,000 denarii as stipendium for 1 January 300.

10) The second of two letters (lines 204–207) ordering 93,125 denarii to be paid to the II Traiana's equites promoti as donatives to celebrate the third consulate of the two Caesars, Constantius and Galerius.

11) A letter (lines 245–249) sent on 28 January 300 and received on 26 February in which the Procurator orders paid to the vexillation of legio III Diocletiana under the praepositus Prodianus at Syene 8,280 Italian sextarii of salt and 8,280 pounds of oil as salgamum[13] for the four months 1 September to 31 December 299.

12) A letter (lines 259–265) sent on 28 February 300 and received in early March in which the Procurator orders two payments of 1,097,500 denarii each to be made to the lancearii of the legion II Traiana under the praepositus Tinton at Ptolemais; these payments represented accession and birthday donatives.

13) A letter (lines 266–270) received on 3 March 300 with a similar order for the payment of 526,875 denarii as donatives for the Caesars' third consulate to the vexillation of legio II Traiana under Tinton at Ptolemais.[14]

14) One of the same batch of letters (lines 285–290) as the previous two (dated 28 February 300), in which the Procurator orders salgamum of 3,596 sextarii of salt and 3,596 litrae of oil for the two months 1 November to 31 December 299 to be issued to the lancearii of legio II Traiana at Ptolemais.

15) Another letter (lines 292–298) from the same batch containing an order for the cohors XI Chamavorum under their tribune Ursus at Peamou opposite Abydus[15] to be paid as stipendium for 1 January 300 65,500 denarii, as well as 32,866 denarii as annona for the four months 1 September to 31 December 299.

16) The last letter (lines 299–304) before the papyrus is mutilated, in which the Procurator orders the lancearii of the legion III Diocletiana stationed at Panopolis ('with you') to be paid fifty pounds of silver bullion and 50,000 denarii in coin as a gift from the Tetrarchs.[16]

It is important to stress that nowhere in these papyri, which contain orders for various

---

[7] Skeat (op. cit. [note 1], page 83) mis-translates this as 32,500.
[8] This does appear to be a reference to *equites sagitarii* but it should be noted that the word for 'mounted' ('hippeusi') has been restored by the editor (Skeat, op. cit. [note 1], page 82).
[9] Potecoptos appears to be identical with the Coptos of the **Notitia** (cf. Skeat, op. cit. [note 1], page 145): it is there recorded as housing a unit of *equites sagitarii indigenae* and the legion I Valentiniana (Or. 31, 26 and 36). It has been identified as equivalent to the modern Qebti or Qift.
[10] Modern Tebu. The **Notitia** records it as still housing II Traiana (Or. 31, 34).
[11] It has been suggested that this vexillation is the same as the one from the legions III Gallica and I Illyrica, which is recorded by an inscription of AD 315/6 (**ILS** 8882).
[12] Modern Dendera, where the **Notitia** records one of several units of local horse archers (Or. 31, 25).

[13] Skeat (op. cit. [note 1], page 149) suggests this is 'materials for pickling.'
[14] Skeat (op. cit. [note 1], page 150) suggests the two vexillations of II Traiana (in letters 12 and 13) are different formations; few others have agreed.
[15] 'Peamu' is only otherwise known from the **Notitia** but it must have been situated on the right bank of the Nile, as it is described as opposite Abydus (modern El-'Araba el-Madfuna); the **Notitia** garrison (Or. 31, 61) is the same cohort of Germans.
[16] Skeat (op. cit. [note 1], page 152) suggests this bullion was worth 240,000 denarii.

payments in cash and kind, are any actual unit size details included and all such figures based on the Panopolis evidence are of an inferential nature only. Such statements therefore as 'A papyrus from Egypt ... reveals an ala with about 120 men and a cohort with about 160'[17] need to be approached with great caution. In this field, theory is all too easily codified as fact.

The first coherent examination of these letters and their possible implications came with Jones and his breakthrough discovery that all the donative figures in the papyri were divisible by 625.[18] There are a couple of considerations to bear in mind before examining Jones's assumptions in detail. Firstly, the claim for a donative rate based on multiples of 625 denarii per man seems low, especially in view of earlier recorded donatives of more than 5,000 denarii and the serious inflation of the late third century. A reasonable response to this objection would be that by the time of the Panopolis papyri donatives were no longer occasional gifts (usually granted once a reign – on the accession) but in effect had become a series of regular annual payments. Skeat denies that there is any evidence that donativa were graded according to arm of service or rank[19] but there is in fact a record of an occasion at the beginning of Marcus Aurelius's reign (AD 161) when donatives were paid at different rates for officers and other ranks,[20] and this does not seem unreasonable in view of the very considerable differentials recorded for stipendium rates.[21] Jones's calculations for donative rates are not to be dismissed out of hand but they have certainly not won universal acceptance.

If we could achieve some certainty over individual shares of any of the items listed in the papyri – pay, donatives, annona, or salgamum – then some fairly simple arithmetic would produce concrete figures for the sizes of two alae, a cohort and several legionary vexillations of the Egyptian garrison in AD 299/300. Such certainty unfortunately is not available and we must instead consider the plausibility of various possible alternatives.

Considering the possibilities based on stipendium first, Jones posits an annual pay rate for legionaries and auxiliary cavalry of 600 denarii, usually paid in 200 denarii instalments every four months, while auxiliary infantry received 375 denarii p.a.. Using these figures gives the following sizes for the units referred to in the papyri:–
(a) 367½ for ala I Hiberorum at Thmoö on 1 January 300[22]
(b) 1,716½ for the detachment of the legion III Diocletiana with the governor on 1 January 300[23]
(c) 524 for cohors XI Chamavorum at Peamou.[24]

There is nothing intrinsically unreasonable about these resulting figures but one or two observations need to be made. Jones's pay rate assumptions are compatible with what is known for the period up to the early third century but not enough is known about the situation at the time of the Panopolis papyri to be safe in assuming that these rates still applied. One alternative pay rate suggested for alares rather lower than Jones's would put it at 450 denarii p.a.[25] and this would produce a unit total for I Hiberorum of 490 men. This is not only reasonably close to the nominal strength of a quingenary ala but also matches well with Arrian's widely accepted figure of 512.[26] On the other hand, if the figure of 490 were applied to the annona allowance in the same letter, it would produce the difficult sum of 144½ denarii per man p.a.. The whole issue of fractions remains a problem yet to be resolved for the two major sets of calculations derived from the Panopolis papyri: the only certainty is that the Roman army did not include fractions of men! Jones himself[27] warns that units certainly included men paid above the basic rate (as well as possibly recruits not paid at first, at least as far as donatives were concerned), and that without being able to quantify these differentials, it is impossible to remove the fractions. It should be possible to construct model ala structures which allow for whole number solutions however: assume, for example, an ala of 354 men of whom 339 were paid at the basic rate but also including 12 duplicarii (3.4%) and three sesquiplicarii (0.9%) and Jones's assumed pay rate of 200

---

[17] P.A. Holder, **The Roman Army in Britain**, 1982, page 98.
[18] A.H.M. Jones, **The Later Roman Empire 284–602: A Social, Economic and Administrative Survey**, Oxford, 1964, Chapter 17, note 31=Volume 3, pages 187–189.
[19] Skeat, op. cit. [note 1], page xxviii.
[20] **SHA**, Marcus Antoninus, 7, 9.
[21] Cf. G. R. Watson, **The Roman Soldier**, London, 1969, pages 91–101.

[22] Letter 2: 73,500 ÷ 200 = 367.5.
[23] Letter 3: 343,300 ÷ 200 = 1,716.5.
[24] Letter 15: 65,500 ÷ 125 = 524.
[25] P.J. Casey, **Roman Coinage in Britain**, Aylesbury, 1980, page 49.
[26] See Chapter 1, page 2.
[27] Jones, loc. cit. (note 18).

denarii per four months would divide into 73,500 denarii exactly.[28] Although other models could be proposed, the above is of the same order as XX Palmyrenorum appears to have been: P. Dura 100 records some 2-3% duplicarii in the unit, while P. Dura 82 records approximately 1.6% duplicarii and 0.5% sesquiplicarii.[29] 354 is also the figure which matches exactly with the annona allowance in the same letter on the basis of this amounting to 200 denarii per annum.[30]

A similar exercise may be carried out with the second stipendium payment, the 343,300 denarii paid to a vexillation of III Diocletiana. Leaving untouched Jones's 200 denarii basic pay scale but allowing for small proportions of troops being paid at 1½ times and double that rate, the fraction can be removed while still ending up with a detachment of about 1,700 men: a total of 1,690 legionaries, for example, would receive exactly 343,300 denarii if 1,658 were paid at the flat rate, 21 (1.2%) at double and 11 (0.7%) at 1½ times.[31]

This fine tuning of Jones's calculations about stipendium to remove the unconvincing fractions would, in other words, produce the following unit size conclusions:
(a) cohors XI Chamavorum could still be considered as possibly 524 strong;
(b) ala I Hiberorum seems more likely to have been 354 strong; and
(c) the vexillatio of the legion III Diocletiana could be adjusted downwards slightly to perhaps 1,690.

Jones claims that 'Donatives are the simplest'[32] payment to quantify and proposes the following rates:-
(i) 2,500 denarii for an officer for the birthday or accession anniversary of an Augustus;
(ii) 1,250 denarii for a legionary on the same occasions;
(iii) 625 denarii for legionaries for the consulate of a Caesar (or Caesars); and
(iv) 250 denarii for auxiliaries.

Although consulate donatives were obviously occasional payments, birthday and accession payments were not and amounted to a regular bonus substantially larger than the stipendium rates, which were very possibly still the Severan levels - a century or so old by the time of the Panopolis papyri (and that a century of rapid inflation). Jones calculates the income from donatives to have been as much as 7,500 denarii p.a. for legionaries in years when the emperor was consul, and 1,250 for auxiliaries.

The horse archers in letter 4 above (Jones's D & E) would have numbered 242, if this donative were paid at the highest 'legionary' rate of 1,250 (although this is not actually a legionary detachment[33]). The dromedary unit, ala II Herculia, in letter 5 above (Jones's F & G) would have had only 215 men if paid at Jones's lowest 'auxiliary' donative rate of 250 denarii.[34] The various legionary detachments in Papyrus 2 would have had strengths of 1,109 (letter 6/Jones's H: II Traiana); 1,997 (letters 7 & 8/Jones's I & J: 'various Eastern legions')[35]; 149 (letter 10/Jones's N: equites promoti of II Traiana); 878 (letter 12/Jones's P & Q: lancearii of II Traiana); and 843 (letter 13/Jones's R: lancearii of II Traiana again[36]). The calculations for letters 10 and 13 use the lower 'consulate' donative calculation of 625 denarii: if the higher figure of 1,250 is applied, fractions result.

Jones states that he sees the key to examining the annona payments in the document he calls U (letter 15) where the cohors XI Chamavorum received, in addition to its four months' stipendium payment for 1 January 300, 32,866 denarii as annona for the last four months of 299. Jones claims that the latter figures '... can hardly represent anything but 493 men at 66 2/3 ... , i.e. 200 denarii a year ....'[37] Applying this rate to letter 2, produces the figure for the ala of 354 already discussed above where an attempt has been made to produce a standard unit size based on both stipendium and annona payments. The cohort at Peamou however is left apparently with 524 recipients of stipendium but with only 493 soldiers being paid annona. This apparent discrepancy of 31 men between the two payments in the same letter is not easy to explain. It may be that some troops were entitled to one payment but, for some reason, not the other;[38] it could be that this year-end period saw the discharge of time

---

[28] 339 x 200 + 12 x 400 + 3 x 300 = 73,500.
[29] **P. Dura** 100 lists some 29 or thirty duplicarii; **P. Dura** 82 lists 15 plus five sesquiplicarii.
[30] Letter 2: 23,600 ÷ 354 = 66.666.
[31] 1,658 x 200 + 21 x 400 + 11 x 300 = 343,300.
[32] Jones, loc. cit. (note 18).

[33] A rate of 625 denarii would put the detachment at 484 men; one of 250 denarii would put it at 1,210.
[34] Jones miscalculates this as 211.
[35] Jones miscalculates this as 1,981.
[36] Skeat (op. cit. [note 1], page 150) assumes these are two different units of lancearii, even though they have the same commander.
[37] Jones, loc. cit. (note 18).
[38] Could they have been new recruits yet to be paid *stipendium*?

expired veterans from the unit but this would only make sense if stipendium was paid in advance rather than in arrears;[39] or, of course, it might be the case that either the stipendium assumption of 125 denarii or the annona assumption of 66 2/3 is wrong – or both could be wrong.

In conclusion, Jones's interpretations of the Panopolis papyri could be extrapolated to suggest early fourth century unit sizes as follows:-
(a) alae of some 200-350;
(b) cohorts of about 500; and
(c) legionary vexillations in the region of 1,000.

Fourteen years after Jones's work was published, R.P. Duncan-Jones re-assessed the Panopolis papyri in a short paper[40] whose conclusions have become very influential and quite crucial to most contemporary interpretations of Late Roman Army unit sizes. Duncan-Jones's starting point is the area of the Panopolis papyri largely ignored by Jones, the payments in kind. The centre of his thesis relates to the two letters in the first Panopolis papyrus ordering payment to ala I Hiberorum at Thmoö of 2,610 Italic modii of barley and 128 7/8 artabas of wheat for the sixty days 29 August-27 October 298. It seems reasonable to assume that these items represent respectively fodder for the unit's mounts and a bread ration for its troopers.

In summary, Duncan-Jones's argument is that 1 artaba = 4.5 modii; 1 modius = 8.6185 litres; a daily fodder ration was 3.2 litres per horse; and that the strength of ala I Hiberorum therefore was 116 horses (and also 116 men).

A sixth century military document[41] gives a fodder ration of apparently 3.2 litres per horse per day, although Duncan-Jones allows that there are contradictory references too.[42] He takes this sixth century allowance to calculate a ration strength for the Thmoö garrison of 116 men.[43] Of course, 116 mounts need not imply 116 troopers and, it could be argued, is implicitly unlikely. Any remount capacity would of course reduce the size of the ala still further (10% remounts would mean only about 104 men) but all Duncan-Jones's calculations, it should be noted, require a 1:1 ratio of horses to soldiers.[44]

These assumptions would put the wheat allowance for the Thmoö troops at 0.7182 litres of bread per man per day (about 2.2 pounds). Duncan-Jones himself admits that this quantity (totalling 2½ modii of wheat per man per month)'... is relatively low'[45] but his case involves rejecting other interpretations of the dry measures involved. He had earlier[46]

---

[39] In theory a service period of 25 years might leave a unit expecting to retire 1/25 of its strength each year but a relatively low life expectancy would increase this considerably in practice, perhaps to more like 1/12 (R. Tomlin, **pers. comm.**). 31 veterans is reasonable on this basis (about 1/17) but perhaps the cohort had also recruited heavily in AD 275 to replace combat losses caused by the Palmyrene invasion of 269/71 and/or the Alexandrian revolt of c. 272. Yann le Bohec, however (**The Imperial Roman Army**, London, 1994 [originally published as **L'Armée Romaine sous le Haut-Empire**, 1989], page 229) implies a military life expectancy – based on evidence from the legion III Augusta – in the mid-40s; this would allow an average soldier recruited in his early 20s to approach very near to the end of a quarter century of service.
[40] R.P. Duncan-Jones, 'Pay and Numbers in Diocletian's Army', **Chiron**, Band 8 (1978), München, pages 541-60. A revised version was published as chapter 7 of Richard Duncan-Jones's **Structure and Scale in the Roman Economy**, Cambridge, 1990, pages 105-17.

[41] **P. Oxy.** 2046.
[42] Polybius, for example, refers to cavalry under the Republic being given 12.1 or 8.6 litres of barley per day (**Histories**, 6, 39): the two different measures were for Roman and allied cavalry respectively. Polybius's measure is usually reckoned as equivalent to 1.6 kilos [3½ pounds]: this level of fodder is supported by a sixth century papyrus (**P. Oxy.** 2046).
[43] 2,610 modii for two months (60 days) at a rate of four choenices = 3/8 modius per horse (2,610 ÷ 60 x 8 ÷ 3) = 116. R.W. Davies ('The Supply of Animals to the Roman Army and the Remount System', **Latomus** Tome 28, Brussels, 1969, pages 429-59) calculates an ala strength at Thmoö of about 107 on the basis of allowing 2.7 artabas per horse per month following **P. Amh.** 107 (published as No. 387 in A.S. Hunt and C.C. Edgar [edd.], **Select Papyri** Volume 2, Loeb, London, 1963, pages 490-1), which records the receipt in AD 185 of 20,000 artabas of barley as an annual allowance for the ala Heracliana at Coptos. Davies assumes the regiment had 600 mounts. M.A. Speidel [1992, page 99] uses the stipendium payment to suggest a maximum strength for the ala of just 105 men.
[44] J.M.C. Toynbee (**Animals In Roman Life and Art**, London, 1973, page 341) takes the Polybian ration scales as implying that each trooper was required 'to maintain three horses and two attendants.' There is nothing intrinsically unreasonable in these figures.
[45] Duncan-Jones, 1978, page 543. Robert O. Fink (**Roman Military Records on Papyrus**, Philological Monographs of the American Philological Association No. 26, Cleveland, 1971) cites a series of second and third century records showing a monthly grain ration to troops in Egypt of one artaba per man (Nos. 78, 79 and 81). It has also been pointed out – and the grain rations are at the heart of Duncan-Jones's thesis – that the 2.5 modii per month ration has been calculated ignoring what appears to be an additional allowance ordered in another letter of the same date (**P. Beatty Panop.** 1, 399) of a further 100 artabas of wheat: cf. Constantine Zuckerman, 'Legio V Macedonica in Egypt: CPL 199 Revisited', **Tyche**, 3 (1988), pages 279-87, footnote 23.
[46] R.P. Duncan-Jones, 'The Choenix, the Artaba and the

argued at length for new Roman and Egyptian dry measure sizes, putting the modius at 8.6185 litres (not 8.75 or 8.67 litres, as claimed earlier) and 4½ modii as equivalent to 1 artaba. Skeat, on the other hand, worked on a figure of 1 artaba = 3.33 or 3.25 modii and this would put the wheat rations for a 116 man ala at about 0.53 litres (or 1.6 pounds) per man per day. At least one other artaba:modius equivalent is known (1:5)[47] and this would again alter the calculations (and consequently the size of the Thmoö ala). In addition there is some evidence for both fodder and food rations different from those resulting from Duncan-Jones's calculations: Polybius, for example, cites fodder rations three or four times larger[48] than the 3.2 litres of barley a day suggested above, while one artaba of wheat per man per day is attested for the Principate.[49] Duncan-Jones however seems attracted by the neatness of two months' rations amounting almost exactly to five modii per trooper and five artabas per mount.[50]

These considerations will need to be borne in mind when examining the rest of Duncan-Jones's argument in detail. Turning to the next letter (2), Duncan-Jones rejects Jones's argument for annona of 66 2/3 denarii per man per four months (200 denarii per annum) since this estimate, as we have seen, would put the ala at a strength of 354. Although conceding that an increase in 16 months of 238 men over his own calculation of 116 (a threefold rise in numbers) '... is conceivable',[51] he argues that the 'lesser hypothesis' would be for the unit to have remained more or less static in size but for a different annona rate to have applied. Duncan-Jones's assumption is for annona three times higher: 600 denarii per man per year, which would produce exactly 118 shares.[52] He then goes on to argue that the stipendium was similarly three times higher than Jones reckoned: at 1,800 denarii p.a. the number of shares would have been 122½.[53] Duncan-Jones explains the mismatch with his annona result by allowing for a few payments above basic for higher grade troops. His conclusion are that the ala at Thmoö was 116/118 strong in 298/300, and that alares were paid a total of 2,400 denarii a year in pay and donatives.

There are some problems with Duncan-Jones's conclusions about remuneration. He concludes that Diocletianic legionaries were paid 12,400 denarii per annum, made up of 1,800 as stipendium together with annona of 600 denarii and 10,000 denarii in donatives. This assumes that alares were paid the same as legionaries but it is not certain that this was the case in the first and second centuries. This total of remuneration would incidentally have made legionaries five times better paid than the highest wage recorded in Diocletian's price edict of AD 296 – the 2,400 denarii p.a. for Greek, Latin and geometry teachers.

A couple of other points need to be made at this stage. Although there is no reason to suppose that the last known pay scales still applied in c. 300[54], it seems that auxiliary cavalry were paid 450 denarii p.a. under Caracalla (quoted, for example, by P A Holder, **The Roman Army in Britain**: Table 1, page 143). This rate applied to the stipendium sum in letter 2 produces the intriguingly exact ala size of 490.[55] We might also wonder whether Duncan-Jones's figures do not leave the Thmoö unit rather **too** stable with

---

Modius,' **Zeitschrift für Papyrologie und Epigraphik** Band 21 (1976), Bonn, pages 43–52.
[47] **Metrologicorum scriptorum reliquiae** I.224.13 & 245.28.
[48] Cf. note 42. Donald W. Engels (**Alexander the Great and the Logistics of the Macedonian Army**, Berkeley, 1978) quotes a range of fodder scales from 0.68 kilogrammes [1.5 pounds] per day (Xerxes' troops), through 1.36 kilogrammes [three pounds] (the US Civil War) to 3.06 kilogrammes [6.75 pounds] (the Spartans); a modern calculation would be for a horse doing moderate work to be given 9–11 kilogrammes [20–24 pounds] a day, half in grain and half in forage. This is much the same as the fodder rations allowed by the Wehrmacht up to 1943: an infantry division was supplied with 53 tons per day for its 5,375 horses (i.e. 9–10 kilogrammes [20–22 pounds] per horse). Duncan-Jones's 3.2 litres is equivalent to about three kilogrammes [seven pounds] per horse per day. Colin M. Wells ('Where Did They Put the Horses? Cavalry Stables in the Early Empire,' **Limes: Akte des XI. Internationalen Limeskongresses**, Budapest, 1977, pages 659–65) states that horses of 12–14 hands would have required 1.6 kilogrammes [3½ pounds] of barley per day plus 4.5 kilogrammes [10 pounds] of hay and green forage. Ann Hyland (**Equus: The Horse in the Roman World**, London, 1990) agrees that the Polybian allowance of 3½ pounds of barley, if supplemented with ten pounds of hay, would have sufficed for small horses engaged in very moderate work and makes the interesting observation (page 41) that ancient grain had a higher nutritional value than modern (about 20% for barley compared with about 11% in modern times).
[49] Cf. note 45 (Fink).
[50] Duncan-Jones, 1990, page 108.

[51] Duncan-Jones, 1978, page 543.
[52] $23,600 \times 3 \div 600 = 118$.
[53] $73,500 \times 3 \div 1,800 = 122.5$.
[54] When there had been some eighty years of rapid inflation. Nicholas Higham (**Rome, Britain and the Anglo-Saxons**, London, 1992, page 43) estimates that prices rose by nearly 1,000% between the 190s and the 260s. Duncan-Jones (1990, page 115) calculates that stipendium had risen only six times however between the reigns of Domitian and Diocletian.
[55] $220,500 \div 450 = 490$.

only two more soldiers (fewer than 2%) present after well over a year. The Twentieth Palmyrenes at Dura 60-80 years earlier seems to have a positively unstable strength in comparison. It seems, for example, to have lost the equivalent of nearly half that 2% in just three days, while the unit total for the latter date (27 March 223/235) is 131 men (or more than 14%) lower than the lowest suggested total recorded perhaps as little as three years earlier.[56] It is also worth considering whether Duncan-Jones might have been correct about the provision measures (which put I Hiberorum at 116 on 24 September 298) but wrong to reject Jones's donative assumption of 200 denarii p.a. in favour of a figure three times higher. Although an increase from 116 to 354 over a year and a third is indeed large, it would still leave the unit at only about 69% of a nominal quingenary ala strength of 512 – and the increase did follow a period of invasion and uprising in Egypt. Could it be that I Hiberorum had suffered heavy casualties in the rebellion of Domitius Domitianus in AD 297/8 and that these casualties had been partly made up by the beginning of 300?

One of only two other items of stipendium evidence in the Panopolis papyri (apart from the individual payment to an officer in letter 9) is an amount of 343,300 denarii to a detachment of legionaries of III Diocletiana in the 'office' of the praeses of the Thebaid for 1 January 300. Jones's calculation for pay had put this vexillation size at an unconvincing 1,716½ but Duncan-Jones's estimate of 572 1/6 is hardly more felicitous.[57] The third stipendium record from Panopolis refers to 65,500 denarii paid to the men of cohors XI Chamavorum at Peamou for 1 January 300. Duncan-Jones rejected Jones's estimate for this unit of 524 men in favour of 163½ on the basis of each soldier being paid 1,200 denarii p.a..[58]

Duncan-Jones then looks at the donative evidence from Panopolis. He claims that the 2,500 denarii (or 10,000 sesterces) payment to the officer of legio II Traiana in letter 9 represented what he called a 'Type A' rate paid to all legionary and cavalry ranks on occasions relating to the Augusti. He also proposes a 'Type B' rate (for commemorations in regard to the junior Tetrarchs) of 1,200 denarii also paid to all ranks. It is ironical however that one of the sources Duncan-Jones cites as supporting his proposed scale of donatives is the reference to the **SHA** Life of Marcus Aurelius which tells of 20,000 sesterces 'each for the other ranks' but 'the rest (sc. receiving) proportionately more.' It may well be then that, even if there were different sorts of donatives for different occasions, differentials rather than flat rates operated anyway.

Part of Duncan-Jones's case against Jones's suggested donative multiplier of 625 (denarii) is that it appears to give one unit a 'shifting membership'. The lancearii of legio II Traiana at Ptolemais would have numbered, according to Jones, 878 on 22 December 299 but only 843 on 1 January 300. Duncan-Jones prefers to argue instead for a static sized unit but with the two payments being at his Type A and Type B levels: the Ptolemais detachment would then have a fixed size of 439 men. It might be noted that the apparent loss to the unit resulting from Jones's 625 denarii calculation amounts to only 4% over ten days, and it might be suggested as more than a coincidence that this reduction occurred over a period including the end of a year (AD 299); it is again possible that the unit was discharging its time-expired veterans.[59]

Duncan-Jones's own donative reckoning however creates its own difficulties – notably some strikingly tiny units. The II Traiana detachment at Tentyra, for example, he puts (based on his 'consular' donative figure of 1,200 denarii) at just 77.604 men, while ala II Herculia Dromedariorum at Toëto and Psinabla (based on the higher donative rate of 2,500 denarii) would have contained just 21 soldiers! Although it is the Thmoö ala, with an establishment of just under 120 by these calculations, which has become something like an assumed norm for Late Empire cavalry units, there is no logical reason why it should be seen

---

[56] Cf. Fink, **RMR**, Nos. 47 and 50.
[57] The known Caracallan legionary pay rate of 675 denarii p.a. would however put this detachment at 1,525.8: 343,300 x 3 ÷ 675 = 1,525.777.
[58] One calculation for pay rates in the early third century (Casey, loc. cit.) would put the differentials between legionaries and *cohortales* at 3:1, rather than the 2:1 assumed by Duncan-Jones. Allowing the latter's assumption that legionaries were paid 2,400 denarii but assuming the auxiliary infantry of cohors XI Chamavorum were paid only one-third of this would increase the unit size to 245.6 men: 65,500 x 3 ÷ 800 = 245.625. M.A. Speidel [1992, page 99] has proposed an even smaller cohort of 131 men or fewer.

[59] Cf. note 39. The diploma evidence for auxiliaries seems to show that discharges could be granted at any time but it seems at least possible that the men might actually be retained beyond their discharge dates to the end of the calendar year or at least that the unit could carry their names and receive payments for these 'ghost' troops. It is no doubt mere coincidence that the 35 men Jones's figures would imply the detachment lost in ten days represents almost exactly the 1/25 which theory would require it to shed annually.

as any more typical than II Herculia Dromedariorum – except perhaps that formations under two dozen strong (in this case split between two bases!) are extremely difficult to envisage. This type of strength would, after all, represent only some 4% of Arrian's ala of 512.

Duncan-Jones then turns his attention to the oil and salt allowances in the papyri. Having already proposed a size for the legionary vexillation at Ptolemais of 439 men, he then needs to establish ration sizes from that basis. The oil allowance (3,596 sextarii for sixty days) would give 439 soldiers 1/11 of a sextarius (57 grammes or just over two ounces) per man per day.[60] He claims that this is close to 'an attested rate' from a sixth century papyrus but admits that this 1/11 allowance related specifically to summacoi ('allies' or possibly 'messengers') while troops were allowed 1/8 of a sextarius.

Duncan-Jones largely ignores the salt allowance in letter 14 of 3,596 pounds of salt but his assumption that the unit had 439 men would have given each man about 85 grammes [three ounces] of salt a day. This seems a very high allowance but it is not clear exactly what salgamum was: could it have been garum (fish sauce) or a substitute for that, or was it intended to be used for preserving meat?[61]

The various legionary detachments referred to in the Panopolis papyri can also be assessed using Duncan-Jones's calculations for payments in cash and kind: his overall conclusion is that these were normally some 500-600 strong (or about half the size assumed by Jones). The 2,500 denarii ('Type A') donative rate applied to the II Traiana element at Apollonopolis Superior, for example, produces a strength of 554½, while the salgamum allowance, calculated according to Duncan-Jones's 1/11 of a sextarius rate for oil, applied to a vexillation of III Diocletiana at Syene puts that formation at 506 strong.

Certainly the results of such estimates would imply legions of this period – at least in Egypt – very much smaller than the 5,000 or so men usually assumed for the Principate.[62] II Traiana, for example, would number no more than just under 1,100 men according to Duncan-Jones: 554.5 at Apollinopolis Superior, 439.5 (the lancearii) at Ptolemais and 77.6 (the equites promoti) at Tentyra.[63] This legion had been in Egypt for well over 150 years at the time of these documents and it seems safe to assume that most, and possibly all, of its strength is represented in these records (although the Notitia [Or. 28.19] also records it at a fourth station – Parembole in the Delta). It is worth recalling that cohors XX Palmyrenorum at Dura just two generations earlier could deploy up to as many as perhaps 1,054 men – or 98% of the size of the legion II Traiana according to Duncan-Jones's estimate.

A similarly small legio III Diocletiana is produced by Duncan-Jones's calculations: about 1078 1/6 split between those with the governor of the Thebaid (572 1/6) and those at Syene (506). There is also however a reference to the lancearii of this legion at Panopolis itself[64] but no certain calculation of the size of this detachment is possible. It seems at least possible however that the Panopolis papyri do not include references to the whole of III Diocletiana, which is recorded in the Notitia at four stations (as well as a permanent detachment in Thrace).[65]

Even accepting Duncan-Jones's suggestions in full with their implication of Diocletianic legions numbering no more than about 1,100 (less than a quarter the size of the usual estimate for the Principate), this does not oblige acceptance of his proposal for a legionary vexillation norm of 500-600. In support of this argument, he also cites: second and third century inscriptions apparently recording 1,000-strong vexillations only because they were above the norm; the Panopolis reference to a vexillation at Potecoptus which Duncan-Jones himself calculates at just under 1,000 men but interprets as a double-sized vexillation from two legions; John Lydus's claim of a 500-strong vexillatio; and Hyginus's reference to a unit with 600 vexillarii.[66]

Support for Duncan-Jones's vexillation proposal as being a reality, if not an official

---

[60] If the 1/8 of a sextarius allowance is applied here, the strength of the Ptolemais detachment would fall to 319 men.
[61] R. Tomlin, **pers. comm.**.
[62] See Chapter 1, pages 1-2.
[63] Total = 1,071.6.
[64] Letter 16: **P. Beatty Panop.** 2, line 301.
[65] Viz. Andros under the *comes limitis Aegypti* (**Notitia Dignitatum** Or. 28, 18), Ombos, Praesentia and Thebes in the Thebaid (ibid. Or. 31, 31, 33 and 38), and at Thebes in Thrace under the *magister militum per Thracias* (Or. 8, 36). [Ombos and Praesentia may in fact have been the same place.]
[66] ILS, 2726 and 531; **P. Beatty Panop.** 2, lines 186-90; John Lydus, **De magistratibus** 1, 46; and Hyginus, **de metatione castrorum**, 5.

norm, has come in a recent article by Constantine Zuckerman, which is however generally critical.[67] An Egyptian papyrus, apparently dating from 18/19 March AD 399 records payments of annonae to a detachment of legio V Macedonica at Memphis. 835 rations of wine (each of one sextarius or 0.54 litres [0.9 pints]) and meat (0.45 kilogrammes [one pound] each) were to be paid apparently for two days, giving a detachment size of about 340-400 men. (This calculation is incidentally dependent on assuming that a fraction of soldiers received multiple annonae.)

It may well be however that this whole search for a legionary vexillation 'norm' is illusory. The word itself has no more precise meaning than 'detachment' in British military usage, 'detail' in US or perhaps Abteilung in German. Duncan-Jones's argument is not, in any case, overwhelming: the Potecoptus vexillation is described as made up from 'various Eastern legions' and it may be true that this means III Gallica and I Illyrica but it is by no means evident that this is a double vexillation. Moreover John Lydus – hardly a military expert – referred specifically to 'vexillationes of 500 **horsemen**' and was not therefore even referring to legionaries. In any case, Duncan-Jones really is being selective with his sources to use this reference while presumably rejecting the relevance of Lydus's references to cohorts of 300 (more than twice his claimed norm) or alae of 600 (five times the norm derived from Duncan-Jones's calculations).

Table 4 below shows the two major interpretations of the evidence of the Panopolis papyri, those of Jones and Duncan-Jones, together with some of the other possibilities discussed above.

Table 4: Some Possible Unit Sizes in Egypt in c. AD 300

Unit Type	Jones	Duncan-Jones	Others
Legionary	1,716½	572 1/6	1,690
vexillations	1,035	506	
	?	?	
	1,109	554½	
	149	77 2/3	
	843/878/899	439<½>	
	1,997	998½	
Alae	354/367½	116/118	104/122½/490
	215	21½	
Cohortes	493/524	163½/164 1/3	
Equites	242	121	

[67] Zuckerman, op. cit. (note 45).

We are left then with interpretations showing two different orders of establishment for the units concerned: Jones's calculations put the units not unreasonably far from the usual estimates for the Principate (although with cavalry units rather weaker), while Duncan-Jones has produced figures showing drastically smaller sizes for all types of units. The latter quantities seem in general to have become the preferred interpretation with most authorities.

Although others have not always been so judicious, it is interesting to note that Duncan-Jones himself warned: 'Evidence from a single province at a particular date need not always reflect practice in the empire as a whole.'[68] There is in fact good reason to place the Panopolis evidence in the context of certain factors quite particular to Egypt in the 290s.[69] This decade had seen two military campaigns there, both subsequent on rebellions: (1) a revolt in late 293 or early 294 involving the towns of Busiris and Coptos, when elements of the legions IV Flavia, VII Claudia and XI Claudia were sent to Egypt, and (2) the uprising of Domitianus in 297-8, which may have involved the whole country at least for a while and during which Diocletian visited Egypt. Mention has already been made of the possibility that some at least of the units referred to in the Beatty Panopolis papyri may have still been under-strength as a result of casualties during one or other of these campaigns. The visit of Diocletian (AD 298/9) seems to have been connected with a major re-drawing of the southern frontier, when pressure from the Blemmyes (the modern Beja, who are recorded raiding during the reign of Probus [267-82]) led to a withdrawal to the First Cataract and the apparent handing over of some territory to a new client area controlled by the Nobatai (Nubians). Philae (the modern Aareq, just above Aswan) became – at 24°N – the southernmost point of the Roman Empire with the new legion I Maximiana stationed in a fort on an island there.[70] Bowman has put the number of legionary troops in the Thebaid at about 10,000 based on Duncan-Jones's estimates (including all of the new legions I Maximiana and III Diocletiana, and vexillations from II Traiana and at least two other

[68] Duncan-Jones, 1990, page 117.
[69] Cf. Alan K. Bowman, 'The military occupation of Upper Egypt in the reign of Diocletian', **Bulletin of the American Society of Papyrologists** 15, 1978, pages 25-38.
[70] **Notitia Dignitatum** Or. 31, 37. Procopius, **Histories** 1, 19, 34 indicates that it was still there in the sixth century.

legions.[71]) but seems less inclined to accept Jones's estimate for 18,000 auxiliaries in Upper Egypt.[72]

The point to stress here is that the Beatty Panopolis papyri reflect a situation in an area of the Empire that had witnessed invasion and rebellion recently, the official response to which seems to have included rationalising the frontier and creating new military posts (such as those at Diocletianopolis, Maximianopolis, Hieracon and Thebes). 'The evidence is consistent with the notion that the main purpose of this activity was to spread the available troops around more thinly and evenly.'[73] This development must have had as much to do with a security or policing rôle as with any strategic or frontier defence function, and this would not necessarily have been the situation in all other provinces.[74]

B: The Notitia Dignitatum

The Notitia Dignitatum is one of the most extraordinary documents to have survived from Roman times. Although some still regard it as the work of an amateur enthusiast with some access to official information, it seems more likely to have been (or to have been derived from) an official document. This information was not always used coherently and the work is riddled with errors and inconsistencies.[75] Although there continues to be much discussion of the date of composition of the Notitia, it is now generally agreed that its two parts are not contemporaneous but that the Eastern section is earlier (written in c. AD 394/5), while the Western part was compiled in c. AD 420-430.

What the information contained in the Notitia should allow us to do – at least in theory – is to construct something like an order of battle for the Late Roman army. The document is essentially a directory of civilian and military offices with details of the responsibilities of post-holders. It provides geographical locations and establishments of the frontier commands, as well as details of the composition of the various field armies. Constant care must be taken to remain aware of the problems of the Notitia – its mistakes, omissions, repetitions and use of material of different dates – but it should nevertheless allow us to speculate on at least the outline of the Late Army and to a certain extent to frame some basic assumptions about possible unit sizes. It would, for example, be relatively uncontentious to take the 188-odd units in the Notitia called 'legions' and to observe the complete impossibility for all these units to have both existed simultaneously (which, of course they may never have done) and to have numbered 5,000 men each – to give a total of nearly a million legionaries[76]: even half that level would seem well beyond the limits of feasibility.

One of the first comprehensive attempts to use the Notitia details to calculate the size of the Roman Army and its individual units in c. AD 400 was that of Várady in 1961.[77] His unit size assumptions were notably complicated: he put most legions at 1,000 but 'riparian' legions at 3,000; cuneii at 1,200; auxilia palatina at 500; and all other formations at 300. This produced figures for the Eastern Army of 96,300 field army troops and 165,700 frontier soldiers (total = 262,000), and for the Western Army of 123,800 field army troops and 107,200 frontier soldiers (total [with certain other additions] = 262,000). These unconvincingly balanced totals put the whole army at 524,000.

A not dissimilar grand total with unit sizes in the same kind of area was adduced by Jones in 1964.[78] His overall total was some 602,000 (plus 6,000 scholae), divided roughly 6:4 between the East and West (352,000: 250,000). The basis for multiplying up the Notitia lists used by Jones was that field army legions numbered 1,000 each and other field army units 500, while frontier formations were of three sizes – 'old' legions at 3,000 each, the few miliary units at nominal size and other formations all 500 strong. Jones's calculations in detail were as follows:–

---

[71] Bowman, op. cit. (note 69), page 32. Note that this figure includes a calculation for the new *legio I Maximiana* of a strength of no fewer than 6,000.
[72] Even Duncan-Jones's assumption (of auxiliary units some 150 strong) would make the **Notitia** Thebaid auxiliaries over 5,000 (35 x 150 = 5,250).
[73] Bowman, op. cit. (note 69), page 32.
[74] There is no evidence, for example, of such sub-dividing (as distinct from outposting) of units in northern Britain.
[75] Further evidence that the **Notitia** was essentially an unofficial document is provided by Robert Grigg's examination of the shield emblems, which are evidently fictional (cf. 'Inconsistency and Lassitude: The Shield Emblems of the **Notitia Dignitatum**', **Journal of Roman Studies** 73, 1983, pages 132-142.)

[76] 188 x 5,000 = 940,000.
[77] L. Várady, 'New Evidences on Some Problems of the Late Roman Military Organisation', **Acta Antiqua Academiae Scientiarium Hungaricae** Tomus 9, Budapest, 1961, pages 333-96.
[78] Op. cit., Volume 3, Appendix 2, pages 379-80.

Eastern Armies

Field army units (51 'legions' at 1,000 + 106 others at 500) = 104,000
Frontier units (29 old legions at 3,000, 13 milliary units + 296 other at 500) [incl. average assumption for omitted Libya] = 248,000

Western Armies

Field army units (45 'legions' at 1,000 + 136 others at 500) = 113,000
Frontier units (15 old legions at 3,000 + 181 others at 500) = 135,500

Jones's totals are of much the same order as the 645,000 of Agathias but, as we have already noted, this latter figure is not easy to accept: it is not clear what period it is referring to, nor whether it is meant as a real statistic from the past or to an ideal 'paper' figure never actually reached in practice. In any event, it would be fair to say that few modern scholars are prepared to accept either Jones's unit size assumptions or the grand totals resulting. MacMullen, for example, - writing a decade and a half later - tentatively suggests a 'Notitia' army significantly smaller at some 400,000: he had suggested a Severan army of about 345,000.[79]

Looking in detail at the mobile forces of the field armies, Tomlin[80] produced a range of possibilities from a total slightly higher than those estimated by Várady and Jones (c. 250,000 cf. 220,100/217,000) down to a much lower figure (c. 130,000). Tomlin calculates the 240 mobile infantry units (127 in the West; 113 in the East) as between 500 and 1,000 strong: the lower figure produces a total of 120,000 men, the higher one of 240,000. Cavalry units, he states, '... were much less than 500 strong': this might suggest between about 17,000 and about 34,000 cavalry in some 85 units (42 in the West, 43 in the East).[81] Even using the lower end of the range for infantry and the higher for cavalry, the proportion of cavalry is low and the actual numbers strikingly so.

The general structural picture provided by the Notitia is, on the whole, very convincing and in harmony with other evidence we have. We can see very clearly, for example, the symmetry in the mobile armies of East and West resulting from a series of divisions in the later fourth century. Tomlin has suggested a very balanced 127 field army units originally in the East and 123 in the West, increased over the course of time to about 157 and 173 respectively.[82]

We can also trace through the Notitia a number of examples of earlier formations surviving into the Late Empire, especially in relatively quiet areas. Margaret Roxan has shown that between 13% and 23% of approximately 410 auxiliary units (c. 310+ cohorts and c. 100+ alae) known from the second century survived to be recorded in the Notitia.[83] These survivals were however very unevenly spread: less then 9% were on the Rhine and Danube but 23% in Africa, 30% in Britain and 36% in the East.[84] The garrisons of north Britain, Egypt, Cappadocia and Raetia in particular contain high proportions of units surviving from the Principate.

The Notitia also reflects a whole series of particular responses to particular situations, some involving frontiers suffering heavy pressure from outside while others (like Britain) were relative 'backwaters' for much of the time. Pragmatic rather than systematic answers would seem to indicate a certain level of intelligence and flexibility from Roman governments. Thus we find, for instance, an exact East-West division of milites (25:25) but with a particular concentration on the lower Danube.[85] On the

---

[79] Ramsay MacMullen, 'How Big was the Roman Imperial Army?' **Klio** Band 62, Berlin, 1980, pages 451-60. He reaches his **Notitia** total (page 458) by applying legionary totals of 1,000 and 400 for other units to Jones's lists. MacMullen's Severan figure (page 452) is calculated on the basis of 34 legions of 5,000 each and the 400 auxiliary units of Eric Birley reduced by 10% to 351 and then assuming these included 10% milliary units, all at 90% of establishment.

[80] Roger Tomlin, 'The Late-Roman Empire' in General Sir John Hackett (ed.), **Warfare in the Ancient World**, London, 1989, pages 222-249.

[81] Ibid, page 238. As illustrative possibilities, five unit sizes are offered:-
85 units x 200 men = 17,000
85 units x 250 men = 21,250
85 units x 300 men = 25,500
85 units x 350 men = 29,750
85 units x 400 men = 34,000.

[82] Roger Tomlin, '**Seniores-Iuniores** in the Late-Roman Field Army', **American Journal of Philology** Vol. 93, 2, 1972, pages 253-78.

[83] Margaret Roxan, 'Pre-Severan Auxilia Named in the Notitia Dignitatum' in R. Goodburn and P. Bartholomew [edd.], **Aspects of the Notitia Dignitatum** BAR Supplementary Series 15, Oxford, 1976.

[84] David Kennedy, 'The East' in John Wacher (ed.), **The Roman World**, London, 1987, pages 266-300.

[85] The units were based in the Thebaid (1), Scythia (8), Moesia Secunda (10), Moesia Prima (5) and Dacia ripensis (1) in the East; and on the Saxon Shore (1) and in Pannonia Secunda (1), Raetia (1), Sequanicum (1), Armorica (9), Belgica Secunda (1) and Mogontiacum (11) in the West.

other hand numeri are very rare: all 15 recorded in the Notitia are stationed in Britain (four on the Saxon Shore and the remainder under the Dux), although it may be only the use of the title that is particularly 'British' as several of these units appear to originate as fourth century field army units while one is very considerably older.[86]

Another example of the obsolete, 'backwater' nature of the British garrison is that most of the Western frontier commands contain no old-style alae at all but of the small total of ten in the West, no fewer than five are in Britain (of which three may have been survivors of the original invasion force of AD 43!).[87] The Eastern frontier commands, on the other hand, contain no fewer than 73 alae of which a startling 32 (40%) were based in Egypt.[88] Like Britain, Egypt according to the Notitia still included many archaic elements: so that, although two of the alae in the command of the comes limitis Aegypti are actually described as 'recently raised',[89] another two units are attested in Egypt in the diploma of 9 June AD 83.[90]

The other 'old-style' auxiliary units – the cohortes – are well spread in the Notitia lists, although the overall total of such units (107) is considerably smaller than estimates for the mid-second century.[91] Most frontier commands contain some cohorts, with Britain again exceptional in having the largest number (38% of the West's total [16]), of which six may have been stationed there since the first century.[92]

Of the newer types of units, very large numbers of equites are recorded in the Notitia frontier command lists (123 units in all). These are reasonably well distributed with most in an arc from Egypt to Armenia and on the upper Danube; there are none in Africa west of Egypt, the lower Danube or the upper Rhine. The type of overall army totals that can be considered feasible argues that this large number of cavalry units must comprise formations individually quite small – nowhere near quingenary size, for instance.

Pragmatism also shows in the way the Notitia records special arrangements in place for particular areas. The lower Danube frontier, for example – comprising the provinces of Scythia, the two Moesiae and Dacia ripensis – includes no alae, no equites and almost no cohorts but instead is defended (in addition to the 'standard' paired legions in each province) by almost entirely new units: cunei (31 of only 47 such formations in the Notitia[93]), auxilia (14 of these rare units[94]) and milites (24 or nearly half of these similarly rare regiments). These new units were presumably recruited for this area to replace earlier losses, incurred particularly during the campaigns against the Goths.

---

[86] It has been suggested [by J.C. Mann, 'Birdoswald to Ravenglass', **Britannia** 20 (1989), pages 75–9] that the first eight numeri in the list of the **Dux Britanniarum** represented part of an early fourth century strengthening of northern defences, including the Cumbrian coast. On the other hand, the Moorish unit at Burgh-by-Sands, *numerus Maurorum Aurelianorum* (**Notitia Dignitatum** Oc. 40, 47), is attested there in the 250s (**RIB** 2042) and may have arrived in Britain half a century earlier with Severus. P. Southern has argued (in 'The Numeri of the Roman Imperial Army', **Britannia** 20 (1989), pages 81–140) that, although it is commonly assumed that *numeri* were small units (of perhaps some 200 men each), there is no real evidence to support this: the archaeological record, for example, includes the 0.6 hectare [1.5 acre] *numerus* fort at Hesselbach in Upper Germany (for some 120–140 troops) but also the Niederbieber fort of 2.1 hectares [5.2 acres]. Southern concludes that 'There was probably great variation ... in individual *numeri*, ranging from about 100 or 150 to about 1000' (ibid, page 104).
[87] Holder (op. cit. [note 17], pages 107 and 110) thinks that *alae I* and *II Asturum*, and *Sabiniana* probably all formed part of Aulus Plautius's expedition.
[88] Since the **Notitia** only lists 83 *alae* in all, the 32 regiments based in Egypt represent no less than 38% of that total! There were, by comparison, only three *alae* in 2nd century Egypt. As well as implying a possible comment on the size and/or efficiency of these units, this contrast also reflects a probable real shift to an increasing emphasis on cavalry on the eastern frontiers. The command of the *dux Palestinae*, for example, contained 60% cavalry units according to the **Notitia**, including two of only four milliary *alae* in the whole Roman army then.
[89] *Alae Theodosiana* and *Arcadiana* (**Notitia Dignitatum** Or. 28, 20 and 21).
[90] *Ala Apriana* and *cohors I Augusta Pannoniorum* (ibid, 32 and 41). Even if this chapter of the **Notitia** dates no later than about the 290s, then these two units had been in Egypt over two centuries.
[91] Eric Birley ('Septimius Severus and the Roman Army', **Epigraphische Studien** 8 (1969), pages 63–82 reprinted in **The Roman Army: Papers 1929-1986** Mavors: Roman Army Researches [ed. M.P. Speidel], Amsterdam, 1988, pages 21–40) reckons there were 270 quingenary and forty-fifty milliary cohorts in *c.* AD 150 (i.e. 310–320 in all). Dr Brian Dobson (in 'The Empire' in Hackett, op. cit. [note 80], pages 192–221) produces figures of a similar order for the same period: 297 cohorts, of which forty were milliary.
[92] *Cohortes I Frisiavonum, I Batavorum, I Tungrorum, II Dalmatarum, I Hispanorum* and *I Morinorum* according to Holder (op.cit. [note 17], pages 114, 116, 118, 119 and 122.
[93] With most of the rest further up the Danube in the two Pannoniae and Valeria. These units may have been formed from *equites* (R. Tomlin, **pers. comm.**).
[94] With all the (ten) other units again further up the Danube in Pannonia II and Valeria. The *auxilia* were probably raised to replace combat losses (R. Tomlin, ibid).

Another area with arrangements quite different from any other is the north African sector equivalent to modern Libya, Tunisia and Algeria (the provinces of Tripolitania, Africa and Mauretania). Here there were apparently a number (38) of geographical commands with each sector commander (praepositus limitis) presumably responsible for a substantial area of desert frontier.[95]

As well as those already cited, numerous other examples of stability (or inertia) in the deployment of forces can be quoted. For example, the Thebaid command in the Notitia may date no later than c. AD 300 but three of the ten cohorts listed there are found in Egypt a century and a half earlier.[96] In Armenia eight of the 21 old-style auxiliary units recorded in the Notitia had survived at least as long, since they are mentioned in Arrian's Hadrianic account.[97] In Moesia Secunda, elements of the legion I Italica[98] are recorded at Novae (modern Cezava?), where it had been based since the late first century, while in the other Moesian province VII Claudia had been at Viminacium (Kostolac) since about the same time and IV Flavia at Belgrade from slightly later.[99] Further up the Danube, the legion II Adiutrix was based at Budapest from AD 114 until an element was recorded still there in the Notitia,[100] which likewise places II Italica at Lauriacum (modern Enns-Lorch, Austria)[101] where it seems to have been stationed for over two centuries (from c. AD 191/205 to c. 451). The details for the command of the dux Raetiae include a number of such survivals including cohors III Britannorum at Abusina (modern Eining, Germany) attested there in 107 and legio III Italica at Castra Regina (modern Regensburg, Germany) since 179. Such inertia could be considered typical of many institutions, not simply of military ones, and could certainly be matched by modern examples. The deployment of both NATO and Soviet forces in Germany, for instance, remained essentially static from 1945 until the recent ending of the Cold War: the British Army's 4th Armoured Brigade is still stationed in north Germany, as it was on V-E Day, while the 9th and 11th Guards Tank Divisions of the former Soviet Army had completed over 45 years of service in the same region when they withdrew. Another example would be the US 2nd Infantry Division, which has served continuously in South Korea from 1965 until the present day and no doubt for many years to come.

At the other extreme, the Notitia lists provide us with the only really detailed evidence to have survived of the sort of disruption caused by long periods of warfare. The command of the dux Syriae et Euphratensis[102] is a prime example of an area where third century battle losses are reflected in a structure dominated by 'new' units: apart from the two legions (IV Scythica and XVI Flavia firma), which had probably been at their bases since before the Severan period, all ten units of equites, both alae and three out of four cohorts were relatively recently formed. It may well be that this type of complexity – reflecting no more than the reality that some frontiers suffered severe disruption, while others remained relatively quiet backwaters – should lead to a search for more complex patterns than the simple assumption that **all** Late Army units were of a similarly small size resulting from similar circumstances. We must also never lose sight of the many internal inconsistencies in our surviving text of the Notitia: for example, the legion V Parthica (which was a casualty of the Persian War of AD 359) has been correctly deleted by its compiler but two other legions lost that year – I and II Parthicae – still appear in the Notitia (Or. 36, 29 and 30) under the command of the Duke of Mesopotamia.

The authenticity of many of the details in the Notitia is further confirmed by the continued survival of units into the fifth century or, in some cases, even beyond: Jones has referred to '... a strong presumption of continuity.'[103] From the command of the Magister Militum Praesentalis II (one of the two main Eastern field armies, normally stationed in Constantinople), the sagittarii Armeni, Daci, Regii and felices Theodosiani are all attested in sixth century Italy, while the Daci and Scythae are found in Egypt in the same era, and the Cornuti (iuniores) had earlier been recorded on Constantinople's Golden Gate inscription.[104] The odd Notitia list for the

---

[95] This whole front covered over 2,000 kilometres [1,240 miles].
[96] *Cohortes I Lusitanorum, scutata civium Romanorum* and *I Apamenorum* (**Notitia Dignitatum** Or. 31, 58-60) are attested in Egypt in 156, 143 and 145 respectively.
[97] *Alae I Augusta Colonorum, I Ulpia Dacorum* and *II Gallorum*, and *cohortes III Ulpia milliaria Petraeorum, IV Raetorum, milliaria Bosporiana, milliaria Germanorum* and *Apuleia civium Romanorum* (**Notitia Dignitatum** Or. 38, 21, 23, 24, 27, 28, 29, 30 and 34).
[98] Ibid, Or. 40, 30.
[99] Ibid, Or. 41, 31 and 30.
[100] Ibid, Oc. 33, 54.
[101] Ibid, Oc. 34, 39.

[102] Ibid, Or. 33.
[103] Jones, op. cit. (note 18), Volume 2, page 655.
[104] The references are: J.O. Tjäder, **Die**

Magister Militum per Orientem similarly includes units which can be traced later: the armigeri seniores Orientales and Transtigritani in sixth century Egypt, the equites tertio Dalmatae under Justinian in Phoenicia, the (legio) prima Isaura sagittaria apparently in late fifth century Egypt and probably the balistarii Theodosiaci in sixth century Palestine.[105] The Theodosiaci stationed in 6th Century Rome[106] were probably either the equites Theodosiaci iuniores recorded in the Notitia under the command of the Magister Militum per Thracias or the seniores under the Magister Militum Praesentalis II.[107] The Notitia records (probably a detachment of) the legion V Macedonica at Memphis (modern Mit Riheina) under the Count of the Egyptian limes, and it remained in Egypt into the late fifth and sixth centuries.[108] Another Egyptian survivor was the cuneus equitum Maurorum scutariorum still apparently at its Notitia base of Hermupolis (modern el Ashmunein) in the early sixth century.[109] Reference has already been made[110] to the astonishing story of the legion IV Parthica, listed by the Notitia under the dux Osrhoenae at Circesium (modern Buseire or Karkisia, Syria)[111] but found at Beroe in Syria in AD 586. Speidel[112] cites archaeological evidence as possibly indicating the survival of the Duke of Arabia's cohors I Thracum at Qasr al Hallabât and legio III Cyrenaica at Bostra (modern Busrâ, Syria) until after 529 and 540 respectively and perhaps even until the Persian and Arab conquests of 613 and 636. As might be expected, these Byzantine survivals from the Eastern lists of the Notitia have no real counterparts in the West. Some survivals can be suggested on the basis of archaeological evidence for the continued occupation of sites[113] but identification with a particular unit is rarely possible: the striking exception is the 9th Cohort of Batavians' continued existence at Passau until c. AD 476.[114]

Ironically enough, the explicit evidence for unit sizes in the Notitia is extremely limited: a few examples based on unit titles or fort names have been cited by Duncan-Jones.[115] None of these examples however is completely convincing. Cohors I centenaria at Tarba (= Thamara: modern Kurnub, Palestine), for example, does sound to have been a 100-strong cohort but the manuscript actually reads agentenaria.[116] In the same way, the unit at Bethallaha in Mesopotamia[117] also appears to have a title indicating its size of 50 men (cohors quinquagenaria Arabum) but Duncan-Jones himself suggests a corruption in the manuscript of the cohort's serial number: the adjacent units in the Duke of Mesopotamia's command are ala secunda, ala octava, ala quintadecima and cohors quartadecima. And, thirdly, the cohort at burgus centenarius in Valeria[118] may well have been 100-strong but is not proved to have been so from the name of its base.

On the other hand, the Notitia does list a small number of units still described as 'milliary'. They are only nine in number (including four alae and four cohorts) and concentrated in a relatively limited area of the East. Three are recorded in Arabia: ala IX milliaria at Avatha; ala II miliariensis at Naarsafari (possibly modern Qasr Bshîr or Khan Qasr el Buleida, Jordan); and cohors I milliaria Thracum at Adtitha (modern Khirbet es-Samra, Jordan).[119] There are three in Armenia: cohors III Ulpia milliaria Petraeorum at Metita;[120] cohors

---

nichtliterarischen lateinischen Papyri Italiens aus der Zeit 445-700, Lund, 1955, 22, 23 (Armeni); ibid, 18-9 (Daci in Italy); Procopius, **Bellum Gothicum**, I, 23 (Regii); Tjäder, op. cit., 16 (felices Theodosiani); C. Wessely, **Studien zur Palaeographie und Papyruskunde**, Leipzig, 1901-, 20, 139 (Daci in Egypt); P. Oxy. 1920, 2046, J. Maspéro, **Catalogue générale des antiquités égyptiennes du Musée de Caire; Papyrus grecs d'époque byzantine**, Cairo, 1911-16 = **P.Cairo** 67002, 67057, P. Grenf. 2, 95 (Scythae); and ILS 9216 (Cornuti).
[105] The references are: **P. Oxy.** 1888 (armigeri); Wessely, op. cit., 20, 131, 139, **BGU** 369 and **Chr.** 1, 471 (transtigritani); Justinian, **Ed.**, 4, 2 (tertio-Dalmatae); Cyril of Scythopolis, **vita Sabae**, 1, 9, 25 (I Isaura); and C.J. Kraemer, Jr., 'Non-literary Papyri' in **Excavations at Nessana, conducted by H.D. Colt, Jr.** Vol. 3, Princeton, 1958, 15 (Theodosiaci).
[106] Tjäder, op. cit. (note 104), 17 and Pope Gregory I, **Epistulae** II, 45.
[107] **Notitia Dignitatum** Or. 8, 27 and Or. 6, 33.
[108] **P. Cairo** 67002 ('Makedones') and G. Zereteli, O. Krueger and P. Jernstedt, **Papyri russischer under georgischer Sammlungen**, Tiflis, 1925-35= **P.R.G.**3, 10 ('Kuntanoi').
[109] Papyri of 502, 507 and 538 record this.
[110] See Chapter 2, page 12.
[111] **Notitia Dignitatum** Or. 35, 24.
[112] M. Speidel, 'The Roman Army In Arabia' in **ANRW** II, 8 (1977), pages 687-730 [reprinted as M. Speidel, **Roman Army Studies** Volume 1, Amsterdam, 1984, pages 229-272], pages 727-8 = 269-70.

[113] Lauriacum (modern Enns-Lorch, Austria) survived until c. 451, while Astura (modern Zeiselmauer or Klosternburg) fell in c. 460+ and Ioviacum (modern Schlögen, Austria) in c. 472+ (**Notitia Dignitatum** Oc. 34, 37, 39 and 45).
[114] Ibid. Oc. 35, 24. See also Chapter 3, page 30.
[115] Op. cit., 1978, pages 553-4.
[116] **Notitia Dignitatum** Or. 34, 40.
[117] Ibid, Or. 36, 35.
[118] Ibid, Or. 43, 62.
[119] Ibid, Or. 37, 25, 28 and 31.
[120] Ibid, Or. 38, 27. Metita has been variously identified with modern Agiyabus, Kale, Tillo or Butan. It was somewhere near modern Malatya on the Euphrates.

milliaria Bosporiana at Arauraca;[121] and cohors milliaria Germanorum at Sisila (Ziziola?).[122] Palestine had two milliary units: ala I milliaria Sebastena at Asuada (modern Khan es Samra) and ala I milliaria at Hasta (modern Wâdi el Khusaiya).[123] And there were the milites milliarienses at Syene (Aswan) in the Thebaid.[124] It may well be of course that these unit titles are of no more than historical significance (perhaps retained through sentiment and pride, or for defining the social or financial status of commanding officers) and had no relevance to the size of the actual formations as recorded in the Notitia: if the correct identification of Naarsafari is indeed the castellum at Qasr Bshîr, this has been described by its excavator[125] as a miniature fort of 0.31 hectares [0.77 acres] built in c. AD 293-305 with stabling for just 69 horses. Milliary alae were never common units but the fort for the only known example in Britain, Stanwix (Uxelodunum), was some 12 times larger than this.[126] It may well be then that apparently 'milliary' units (or at least a proportion of them) were no such thing in the Late Empire but it would then perhaps be wise to reject all the limited direct unit size evidence in the Notitia rather than to make a case from one element of it.

Another consideration that may be of major importance but about which we have only limited information is that the newer units of the Late Army seem to have had a structure radically different from those established under the Principate, and a whole series of new ranks emerged. We can already see from the Notitia that the old titles for unit commanders (legionary legates, prefects for alae and quingenary cohorts, and tribunes for milliary cohorts) were no longer always used in the same way as before.[127] A famous remark of St Jerome[128] lists the ranks for a cavalry regiment as: recruit, trooper (eques), circitor, biarchus, centenarius, ducenarius, senator and primicerius. Such ranks can be seen in use in the Concordia cemetery of perhaps AD 394/5: Flavius Odiscus and Flavius Mamuetus were biarchi of the Brachiati seniores equites and Leones seniores respectively; Flavius Severianus was a centenarius of the equites catafractarii with 22 years service; Flavius Fasta and Flavius Batemodus were ducenarii with the Batavi equites seniores and Heruli seniores respectively; and Flavius Launio and Flavius Hariso were senatores of the same units.[129] The implications of a new rank structure (which seems in any case only to have applied to certain units) for internal unit organisation are not clear but there is also evidence for some retention of traditional make-up too: a dedication by cohorts VII and X of legio II Herculia in perhaps AD 297 might imply that the whole legion with all ten cohorts was still in existence then.[130] We are left then with the problem of how far we can assume that similar or even identically named units did in fact resemble their ancestors. It does not seem to trouble the modern mind greatly that the United States Army of today includes 'cavalry' units (although without horses for at least forty years), that the Dragoon Guards of the British Army operate Chieftain main battle tanks, that the Indian Army still includes Skinner's Horse or the Belgian Army non-cycling 'Carabiniers cyclistes.'

One of the problems arising from the Notitia lists is that, despite the enormous number of frontier and field army units they include, there are still some obvious gaps remaining. A missing page in the Eastern section, for example, (Or. 30) presumably contained the command of the dux Libyarum, while units based in Germania Prima appear to be missing from the Western lists.[131] Also frequently

---

[121] Arauraca is somewhere near the modern villages of Gümüstarlasi and Kavakyolu.
[122] Possible identifications for the site of Sisila (Ziziola) include Öğütlü and Melishan. This stationing of three of only four milliary cohorts recorded in the whole of the Notitia in Armenia is striking. It is difficult to see it as inadvertent and, if a need had been perceived to retain powerful infantry units on a mountain frontier facing the Sassanids, then presumably that purpose would have been degraded had not some effort been made to keep such units somewhere near nominal strength.
[123] Ibid, Or. 34, 32 and 36.
[124] Ibid, Or. 31, 35.
[125] S. Thomas Parker (ed.), 'The Roman Frontier in Central Jordan: Interim Report on the Limes Arabicus Project, 1980-1985' in BAR International Series 340, Oxford, 1987. In a later paper, however, ('New Light on the Roman Frontier in Arabia' in H Vetters & M Kandler [edd], **Akten des 14. Internationalen Limeskongresses 1986 in Carnuntum**, Teil 1, Wien, 1990, pages 215-230) Parker suggests nearly 200 troopers as the size of the garrison.
[126] 3.98 hectares [9.8 acres].

[127] In Britain, for example, the Second Legion (**Notitia Dignitatum** Oc. 28, 19) and the Sixth Legion (ibid, Oc. 40, 18) were commanded by prefects, as were all alae, while all cohorts were under the command of tribunes.
[128] St. Jerome, **contra Iohannem Hierosolymitanum episcopum**, 19.
[129] Dietrich Hoffmann, 'Die spätrömischen Soldatengrabschriften von Concordia' in **Museum Helveticum** 20 (1963), Basle/Stuttgart, pages 22-57.
[130] **ILS** 4195.
[131] See Jones, op. cit. (note 18), Volume 3, Appendix 2, pages 368 and 380, and L. Várady, op. cit. (note 77), page 360.

quoted as an area surprisingly empty of garrison units in the Notitia is western Britain: the whole area from Southampton Water right round the coast to Morecambe Bay was apparently without defences. As this area was under heavy pressure from raiding Scotti from Ireland in the fourth century and later, this seems hard to credit. Unless this threat has been exaggerated (no assault came from the West in the crisis year of 367), could there perhaps have been a western section of the command of the Dux Britanniarum missing from our version or even a separate Count of the 'Scottish Shore' responsible for the defence of Wales and the adjacent part of north-west England?[132]

It may be however that other explanations for apparent gaps in the Notitia or for perceived weaknesses in the Late Army are available. We know that local militias were well established in the Principate: Josephus refers to their use and Tacitus cites a whole series of occasions during the civil wars of AD 69 when locally raised forces were employed - in Gaul, Raetia, Noricum and Mauretania, for example.[133] The Helvetian and Raetian levies appear to have been more than tribal irregulars enrolled for a temporary emergency: the Helvetii were paid and had their own fort, while the Raetians are described as having been well trained. There is every reason to suppose that this pattern continued and some evidence to this effect: the Historia Augusta tells of Didius Julianus, as governor of Gallia Belgica in the 170s, deploying locally raised militia against an invasion of Chauci and a similar use of local levies in Algeria a century or so later.[134] Eric Birley has suggested[135] that the only British auxiliary unit raised from a single tribe, the cohors I Cornoviorum, may have originated as a tribal militia possibly with defence against the Ordovices as its original purpose.

Definitely known to have existed in the Late Empire but also not recorded in the Notitia were the mounted palace guard units known as scholae.[136] R.I. Frank and others[137] have argued that these élite units were created by Constantine as replacements for the now unreliable Praetorians (who had opted for the wrong side) in c. 312/330: they were not part of the regular chain of command but under the Master of the Offices. By c. 400 there were a dozen units of scholae: seven under the Eastern Magister Officiorum and five in the West. They were probably each 500 strong (a total of 6,000) but others have argued for 1,000 each and Frank claims a total of no fewer than 32,500 by AD 527.[138] By the late fourth century, most scholares - in the tradition of Imperial guards units - were Germans and especially Rhinelanders.

Another argument to explain the relative weakness and lack of combat success of the Late Roman Army is the increased use of 'federates': individual barbarians recruited by Roman commanders for the duration of particular campaigns. This case has been put in recent years most strongly by J.H.W.G. Liebeschuetz.[139] There had of course been a long history of assistance to Imperial armies by forces from allies or client kingdoms: Vespasian, for example, deployed in Judea in AD 67 15,000 allied troops in addition to his three legions and 29 auxiliary units.[140] Liebeschuetz sees the foederati playing an even more significant rôle in the campaigns of the late fourth and early fifth centuries. For example, although only two Gothic units are recorded in the Notitia,[141] Jordanes records 20,000 of them fighting with Theodosius

---

[132] Cf. Barri Jones & David Mattingly, **An Atlas of Roman Britain**, London, 1990, Map 4:70, page 139.
[133] Josephus, **Bellum Iudaicum**, 2, 67, 2, 502 and 2, 506; and Tacitus, **Historiae**, 1, 67, 1, 68, 3, 5 and 2, 58. See also Eric Birley, 'Local Militias in the Roman Empire' in **Bonner Historia-Augusta-Colloquium 1972/1974**, Bonn, 1976, pages 65-73 [reprinted in **The Roman Army: papers 1929-1986**, Mavors: Roman Army Researches (ed. M.P. Speidel) Volume 4, Amsterdam, 1988, pages 387-394].
[134] SHA, Vita Didii Juliani, 1, 7 and Vita Gallieni, 13, 8. See also **A.E.** 1928, 38 from Saldae (modern Bejaia/Bougie, Algeria). The Gallienus reference probably refers to the war of 290/3 against the Bavares and Quinguentanei.
[135] Eric Birley, 'Local Militias in the Roman Empire' in **Bonner Historia-Augusta-Colloquium 1972/1974**, Bonn, 1976, pages 65-73, reprinted in **Mavors 4**, pages 387-394, page 393.

[136] The word *schola* originally meant a learned discussion and thus a school or sect.
[137] R. I. Frank, 'Scholae Palatinae: The Palace Guards of the Later Roman Empire' in **Papers and Monographs of the American Academy in Rome** 23 (1969) Rome. See also Roger Tomlin, 'The Mobile Army' in Peter Connolly (ed.), **Greece and Rome at War**, London, 1981, pages 249-59.
[138] Frank, op. cit..
[139] See 'Generals, Federates and Bucellarii in Roman Armies Around AD 400' in Philip Freeman and David Kennedy [edd.], **The Defence of the Roman and Byzantine East: Proceedings of a Colloquium held at the University of Sheffield in April 1986**, BAR International Series 297, Oxford, 1986, pages 463-474 [reprinted in **From Diocletian to the Arab Conquest: Change in the Late Roman Empire**, Aldershot, 1990 as 19], and **Barbarians and Bishops: Army, Church, and State in the Age of Arcadius and Chrysostom**, Oxford, 1990.
[140] Josephus, **Bellum Iudaicum**, 3, 68.
[141] **Notitia Dignitatum** Or. 5, 61 and 6, 61 (*Visi* and *Tervingi*).

against Eugenius in 394 and Orosius claims that 10,000 Goths were killed.[142] The bulk of these Gothic forces must therefore have been temporarily recruited and then disbanded. The need for such barbarian reinforcements is a reflection of the weakness of even Imperial field army units, and they played a significant part in Stilicho's campaigns against Alaric in 397 and Radagaisus in 405/6. There would also of course have been financial advantages to the deployment of temporary rather than regular forces. The recruitment of federate troops led in turn to the development of bucellarii – military retainers of specific commanders. The use of allies only makes sense if Imperial forces were much smaller than the 600,000 or more calculated, for example, by Jones from the Notitia lists: otherwise there '... could hardly have been such need to resort to barbarian federates ....'[143] It is perhaps possible to see this shift away from the use of auxiliary cavalry towards the employment of federates as in some ways a reversion to the situation that had existed in the Republic before the auxilia had developed into a significant element of the regular forces of Rome.[144]

---

[142] Jordanes, **Get**. 145 and Orosius, **Historia contra paganos**, 7, 35.

[143] Averil Cameron, **The Later Roman Empire AD 284–430**, London, 1993, page 147.

[144] See for example Karen R. Dixon & Pat Southern, **The Roman Cavalry: From the First to the Third Century AD**, London, 1992, page 22.

CHAPTER 5

ARCHAEOLOGICAL EVIDENCE

It is possible to compile quite a respectable collection of archaeological evidence for Late Army forts which appears to demonstrate both units of reduced size and sites newly constructed for units smaller than the norms conventionally assumed for the Principate. We will consider firstly the evidence for certain areas of the Empire.

Evidence from the East

In a recent work, Kennedy and Riley[1] have drawn attention to a series of strikingly small forts in the East which seem to equate to sites named in the Notitia as housing conventionally titled auxiliary units. Khan el-Hallabât in Syria, for example, a site on the strata Diocletiana 31 kilometres [19 miles] from Palmyra in the command of the Duke of Phoenicia, was only about 47 metres [153 feet] square and covered just 0.22 hectares [0.55 acres]. This is possibly the same place as the Veriaraca of the Notitia[2] recorded there as the base of ala nova Diocletiana: although a very strong post with massive double walls 3.5 metres [11.5 feet] thick and towers 7.5 metres [24.5 feet] in diameter, it was small – about 10% the size of a typical western fort of the Early Empire.

An even smaller fort was Khan el-Qattar, further down the strata Diocletiana near Homs. It was only some 41 metres [135 feet] square with an area of a mere 0.17 hectares [0.42 acres]. This has been provisionally identified with the Notitia's Cunna or Carneia – base of ala I Francorum.[3] Similar in size was Khan Aneybeh, which stood further south-west along the strata near Homs: it was 48.6 x 39 metres [160 x 128 feet] or 0.19 hectares [0.47 acres]. This site is usually taken to have been the Onevatha or Anabatha, where the Notitia places a unit of 'pacified' Germans: cohors V pacata Alamannorum.[4] Two other small forts in the command of the dux Foenicis are the 0.25 hectare [0.6 acre] Khan as-Sawat, which is probably the Vallis Diocletiana recorded in the Notitia as home of cohors II Aegyptiorum and Khan el-Manqoura near Damascus, a fort of 0.81 hectares [two acres] probably to be equated with the Vallia Alba cited in the Notitia as the base for cohors I Iulia lectorum.[5]

Perhaps the key site for consideration on this frontier is further south in modern Jordan east of the Dead Sea near Al-Kerak: El-Lejjun, widely regarded as being the Betthorus cited in the Notitia as base for the legion IV Martia.[6] This fortress was erected late in Diocletian's reign, probably a little after AD 300 when IV Martia was only about seven years old: it had 2.4 metre [7.9 feet] thick walls, massive corner towers and 20 U-shaped towers each projecting 11 metres [36 feet]. A remark by Procopius[7] has been taken as referring to the disbanding of the legion in c. AD 530, but in any case the regular army probably finally abandoned El-Lejjun after a large earthquake on 9 July 551. It seems to have been substantially reconstructed in the late fourth century following an earlier earthquake in AD 363. Excavation has found a vicus east and south of the fortress complete with mansio, but no praetorium, hospital or latrines have yet been discovered. The fortress measured 242 x 190 metres [790 x 620 feet] and only covered 4.6 hectares [or 11.4 acres]: in contrast an average legionary fortress of the Early Empire would have covered some 18 hectares [45 acres]. Caerleon, for example, was 20.5 hectares [or 50.5 acres].

El-Lejjun's 1980-85 excavators have found eight barrack blocks, each of which could have

---

[1] David Kennedy and Derrick Riley, **Rome's Desert Frontier: From the Air**, London, 1990.
[2] **Notitia**, Or. 32, 34. See also A Poidebard, **La trace de Rome dans le désert de Syrie**, 1934, 48-9.
[3] **Notitia**, Or. 32, 35 and Poidebard, op. cit. (note 2), ibid..
[4] **Notitia**, Or. 32, 41 and Poidebard, op. cit. (note 2), 47, 50.
[5] **Notitia**, Or. 32, 43 and Poidebard, op. cit. (note 2), 43, 54, and **Notitia**, Or. 32, 42 and Poidebard, op. cit. (note 2), 45-6.
[6] **Notitia**, Or. 37, 22. See John Casey, **The Legions in the Later Roman Empire: The Fourth Annual Caerleon Lecture**, Caerleon, 1991, pages 14-15; David Kennedy and Derrick Riley, **Rome's Desert Frontier: From the Air**, London, 1990. and S. Thomas Parker (ed.), 'The Roman Frontier in Central Jordan: Interim Report on the **Limes Arabicus** Project, 1980-1985' in BAR International Series 340, Oxford, 1987 and 'New Light on the Roman Frontier in Arabia' in H Vetters & M Kandler [edd], **Akten des 14. Internationalen Limeskongresses 1986 in Carnuntum**, Teil 1, Wien, 1990, pages 215-230.
[7] Procopius, **Anecdota**, 24, 12-14. It is in fact difficult to see this passage as having quite such a specific meaning: it seems rather to be a far more generalised reference to the down-grading of *limitanei* as regular troops.

held 260 men[8] for a total garrison strength of 2,080 men or just four cohorts. After the earthquake of 363, only half the barracks were rebuilt implying the reduction of the garrison to only slightly more than 1,000 troops. This may reflect the detachment from the legion of two cohorts to serve with Julian's Persian expedition.[9]

A parallel to El-Lejjun is the auxiliary fort of Dionysias (the modern Qasr Qarûn) in Egypt, newly built in c. AD 306 and the base of ala V Praelectorum according to the Notitia.[10] It measured just 83 x 70 metres [272 x 230 feet], some 0.76 hectares [1.9 acres]: British quingenary ala forts, in contrast, averaged some 2.63 hectares [5.8 acres] or 3½ times larger. Another small fort in the Roman East that can be considered is Qdeym in Syria, which has been calculated as only 0.77 hectares [1.9 acres] in size. This has been identified with the Acadama of the Notitia, which housed not a traditionally titled auxiliary unit but one of the numerous units of horse archers found in the Late Army:[11] there were another three such units in the same command of the dux Syriae. This command seems in fact to have suffered very heavy casualties during the third century and very little of its pre-Caracallan garrison survived to be recorded in the Notitia, where most of the Duke's forces (ten out of 16 non-legionary units) were new cavalry units of indeterminate size.[12] We know very little about the establishment of such units, or even if they had standard structures.

The Rhine and Danube

A similar exercise can be carried out further west on the crucial 'northern front' of the Empire, showing both small and reduced forts. Abusina (modern Eining in Germany), for example, base of cohors III Brittonum in the command of the dux Raetiae,[13] was reduced in the fourth century to a 48 x 37 metre [158 x 121 feet] rectangle of about 0.18 hectares [0.4 acres] – only about 10% of the old Trajanic fort's area. In the same command, the new fort for cohors V Valeria Frygum at Piniana (modern Bürgle) was of much the same size and could have held a century or perhaps 150 men at most. Further east in the command of the Duke of Valeria, can be found Intercisa (modern Isny in Hungary, it has been suggested) hosting according to the Notitia three cavalry units (two cunei and a regiment of horse archers) but with space (0.36 hectares [0.9 acres]) apparently for two turmae at most.[14]

Further down the Danube new, small legionary fortresses were built in the Diocletianic period for the recently raised legion II Herculia and legion I Iovia. The former's fortress at Troesmis (modern Iglitsa, Rumania) was a near trapezoid with 150 metre sides covering some 2.8 hectares [7 acres], while the latter's at Noviodunum (modern Isaccea, Rumania) was larger but still covered no more than 5.6 hectares [13.5 acres].[15]

Before turning elsewhere, one or two words of caution are needed about the archaeological evidence considered so far. In the first place, it is important to remember that identification of ancient place names and modern sites is not always easy. Thus, Cunna is only tentatively equated with modern Khan-el-Qattar; Betthorus is very possibly El-Lejjun but no direct evidence has been found from excavation; and Intercisa has also been identified more probably with modern Dunaújváros. Equally it needs to be remembered that the Notitia records represent the freezing of a particular historical situation, which need not necessarily match well with the situation discovered by excavation, or in some cases assumed from aerial or ground surveying.

It is also a significant proviso that Roman Army units seem very frequently to have been subject to detachment of elements from the parent body. This was certainly widespread in all periods but by the Late Empire such

---

[8] Parker estimates each barrack block held four 64-strong centuries with a centurion each: 4 x 65 = 260 x 8 = 2,080.
[9] Parker (1990, page 224) says that the coin evidence supports this suggestion.
[10] Notitia, Or. 28, 34. This is the unit commanded by Flavius Abinnaeus. Dionysias was built in c. AD 306 and, although apparently distant from any external threat, was massively defended with projecting towers and walls 3-4 metres [10-13 feet] thick. [Such defences may also however reflect a new type of prestige spending, past experience of civil war or brigandage, and the fact that such fortifications would in themselves discourage attack whatever the size of the garrison: Professor Peter Salway, **pers. comm.**.] Dionysias was probably abandoned in the late fourth century.
[11] Notitia, Or. 33, 21. See also A. Poidebard and R Mouterde, **Le Limes de Chalcis**, 1945, 109-110.
[12] Four 'Illyrian' units, four units of 'indigenae' (including two of archers) and two other units of horse archers.

[13] Notitia, Oc. 35, 25. The cohort was stationed at Abusina from very early in the second century.
[14] Mark Hassall, unpublished work.
[15] C Scorpan, **Limes Scythiae: Topographical and stratigraphical research on the late Roman fortifications on the Lower Danube**, BAR International Series 88, Oxford, 1980. Notitia, Or. 29 and 32 (but see also 30, 31, 33, 34 and 35).

detachments were increasingly of a permanent nature, and it is at least possible that the smaller sizes of some fourth and fifth century forts simply reflect the recognition of a new or developed reality by military planners and engineers. The ala I Francorum cited above, for example, was stationed not only at Cunna in the Egyptian Frontier command but also 'opposite Apollonopolis' in the Thebaid.[16] Legio IV Martia was apparently responsible for manning, as well as its main base at El-Lejjun, the outposts at Khirbet el-Fityan (a 0.6-hectare [1.5 acre] castellum some 1.5 kilometres [0.9 miles] away) and Rujm Beni Yasser: the recent excavators[17] reckon that the former was capable of having housed over 300 troops. As well as this kind of sub-division among adjacent posts, a practice dating well back into the Principate, Late Army legions were also of course used as a resource from which field army detachments could be created, possibly on an ad hoc basis at first but very frequently made permanent either by design or through inertia. The two mobile units called Martenses[18] presumably originated as such detachments of IV Martia. A similar situation applied to the two Scythian legions cited above: II Herculia was split among two or three sites, while I Iovia was divided among three. It might well be asked whether a Late Army legion was ever, or was ever intended to be, concentrated in one place.

We need also to beware of too readily drawing conclusions from partial excavations or just from fort sizes. At El-Lejjun, for instance, the north-east quadrant of the fort was not fully excavated and the unexplored area may well contain undiscovered evidence for additional occupation.

There is too the problem that even where small forts from the Late Empire do exist, so too quite often do larger ones. A norm for Late Imperial legions (or at least for those raised from the Tetrarchy onwards) of about 1,000 men is now quite a widely accepted concept but it does beg the question of why such a wide range of fort sizes co-existed: even newly raised legions such as the two from the Scythian limes cited above show no real pattern or consistency, as Noviodonum was double the size of Troesmis.[19] It should also be noted that, apart from IV Martia, the other legion in the Dux Arabiae's command (III Cyrenaica) was based at a fort – Bostra (modern Bosrâ eski-Sham, near Dera'a in Syria) – nearly four times larger than El-Lejjun.[20] It is significant in this context that Bosrâ may have been nearly 200 years older than El-Lejjun, and that III Cyrenaica was more than 300 years older than IV Martia (and seems to have provided no field army detachments).[21] Are we again seeing inconsistent evidence merely reflecting an inconsistent reality?

One final factor to consider when seeking to use fort sizes as a criterion for garrison strengths is that very little is known about the possibility of there regularly being upper storeys in the buildings of Roman forts but that they seem to have existed in some instances at least. Kennedy and Riley[22] cite three examples of Jordanian sites with upper storeys: one of these, Deir el-Kahf[23] near Irbid, may be the Speluncae[24] in the command of the Duke of Arabia, which the Notitia records as the base of one of several groups of equites promoti indigenae. Although covering only 0.36 hectares [0.89 acres], the two-storeyed buildings of the castellum could have housed 4-500 men and horses. In the same command, Qasr Bshir (possibly the Notitia's Naarsafari) also had two storeys with ground floor stables and a first floor for the soldiers.

Britain

It is evident that something of a new orthodoxy about Late Roman unit sizes in the British provinces has been developing based on the now well known concept of 'chalets.' The argument for internally altered fort accommodation and thus substantially smaller garrison units originated with John Wilkes's 1960 excavation at Housesteads, and Charles Daniels' interpretation of the findings there as representing married quarters for a greatly reduced cohort.[25]

---

[16] **Notitia**, Or. 31, 51.
[17] Parker (1987).
[18] **Notitia**, Oc. 5, 265 & 7, 91 (in Gaul) and Or. 7, 40 (*seniores* in the East).
[19] 5.6 hectares [13.5 acres] compared with 2.8 hectares [seven acres]: cf. Casey, op. cit. (note 6), page 15.

[20] Bostra measured some 463 x 363 metres (1,520 x 1,190 feet) covering 16.8 hectares [41.5 acres]: very similar in size to IX Hispana's fortress at Lincoln.
[21] Bostra was built in c. AD 106-111. III Cyrenaica was raised in c. 30 BC: cf. Lawrence Keppie, **The Making of the Roman Army: From Republic to Empire**, London, 1984, Appendix 2, page 206.
[22] Op. cit. (note 1). Peter Salway, **pers. comm.**, suggests that Diocletian may have based his retirement home at the palace of Split, where sections of the upper storey are thought to have housed guards and military stores, on the best of current military practice.
[23] = 'monastery of the cave' in Arabic.
[24] = 'Caves.'
[25] J. J. Wilkes, 'Early fourth century rebuilding in

Wilkes had discovered that the standard Hadrianic barrack block XIV at Housesteads with ten contubernia and a centurion's suite had been rebuilt in the fourth century as a series of separate, mostly detached huts with alleys between: he called these buildings 'chalets'. Further excavations at Housesteads by Charles Daniels and John Gillam between 1974 and 1976 revealed a series of six chalets (and a larger two-roomed building) overlying Barrack XIII. Later excavations and the re-examination of older site reports allowed for the extension of the chalet concept to a large number of British forts, mostly in the north.

Rescue work at Wallsend in the mid-1970s showed a re-shaping of eight barrack blocks in the fourth century into new buildings but with fewer chalets than at Housesteads. At High Rochester, two barrack blocks in the western retentura were apparently re-arranged into chalets. Similarly, it appears that the 1894 excavation at Greatchesters revealed five detached chalets together with a larger building. Work at Ebchester in 1972-3 showed a fourth century barrack block rebuilt as two or three back-to-back buildings. Daniels argued from the excavations at Chesters in the 1880s that there were indications that the most southerly of four barrack blocks identified in the eastern praetentura had been not stables but possible chalets. The 1929-31 excavations at Birdoswald showed considerable fourth century rebuilding, including possible chalets, as did both excavation in 1843 and aerial photography in the late 1960s at Risingham.

As well as this quite impressive catalogue of forts on the northern frontier with probable fourth century chalets, Daniels suggested that there may have been chalets also at Caernarvon (where the 1922 excavation showed several possible chalets, mostly undated), Portchester (where possible third or fourth century detached structures were uncovered by work in the early 1970s) and Malton (for which there is a pre-war description of detached fourth century buildings).

Having produced this list of about a dozen forts seemingly rebuilt with chalets in place of traditional barracks, Daniels then looked at the question of whether the new accommodation represented married quarters. Roman soldiers had of course been forbidden to marry until AD 197[26] and, it has traditionally been assumed that even after Severus's 'concession', wives and families would continue to live outside forts probably in vici and that barrack space represented accommodation for military personnel alone. Daniels however took the reconstruction of barrack blocks as discrete living units, together with two other criteria (the presence in forts of typically female objects such as jewellery and the burial of infants) as clear evidence that many forts now contained married quarters. The excavation of Housesteads barrack XIII, for example, produced many brooches and other trinkets, while infant burials have been found at Malton (where pre-war excavation produced 31 bodies of children in 'chalet' floors and a guard-room of the north-east gate) and at Chesters (where two infant burials are recorded in the eastern interval tower of the south rampart).

Daniels concludes that the appearance in the fourth century of chalets in the command of the Duke of Britain was part of a planned Diocletianic or post-Diocletianic reorganisation of the British garrison reflecting the running down and partial abandonment of many Wall forts not just to allow for units to be transferred to the new Saxon Shore defences but also as a result of the permanent reduction of the island's forces during the period of the Gallic Empire. He also attempted to quantify the changed situation on the northern frontier and argued that the Housesteads excavations in the 1960s and '70s indicated only about eighty chalets, while Wallsend contained perhaps 50-52. Assuming that each chalet was assigned to one soldier and his family, the total of accommodation units would therefore also represent the garrison size: in these two instances, the fourth century garrisons would have been about 9.5-10% and about 8.5% of the nominal strength of the known second century units.[27] These are clearly very drastic

---

Hadrian's Wall forts' in M.G. Jarrett and B. Dobson [edd.], **Britain and Rome**, Kendal, 1966, pages 114-138. C. Daniels 'Excavation at Wallsend and the fourth-century barracks on Hadrian's Wall' in W.S. Hanson and L.J.F. Keppie [edd.], **Twelfth Congress of Roman Frontier Studies**, BAR S71, Oxford, 1980, pages 173-193.

[26] Cf. G.R. Watson, **The Roman Soldier**, London, 1969, page 137 and Herodian, 3, 8, 5. C. Sebastian Sommer [**The Military Vici in Roman Britain: Aspects of their Origins, their Locations and Layout, Administration, Function and End**, BAR British Series 129, Oxford, 1984] argues that the prohibition on marriage and therefore the presence of families within forts may have extended also to centurions and decurions.

[27] Daniels, op. cit. (note 25). The garrison unit of Housesteads in the third and fourth centuries (**RIB** 1578 and **Notitia**, Oc. 40, 40) was *cohors II Tungrorum*, a milliary [equitate?] cohort. Eighty men would have represented 9.5-10% of 760-800 men but only 7-8% of the largest possible milliary cohort size (see Chapter 1,

reductions.

Although Daniels did not attempt to expand the chalet concept beyond the sites detailed above (of which he seems to regard just eight as reasonable certainties) and although some north British sites have yet to produce even possible chalet evidence (Ravenglass and Maryport, for example), greater extrapolation has been attempted by others with implications expressed like this: 'Pre-existing barracks were demolished and replaced with terraces of close-set but free-standing 'chalets' ... The capacity of the new-style housing was no more than 15 per cent of that which it replaced, implying the presence of much smaller garrisons, now occupying 'married' quarters. Although widely distributed, the northern command of the Dux Britanniorum [sic] may have been no larger than c. 5000 men, all of whom consisted of the lower-paid frontier troops.'[28] Using traditional unit size assumptions, the old-style cohorts and alae alone in the area of the Duke's command would have totalled more than double this suggestion and, since the Duke controlled two-thirds of all the forces the Notitia assigns to Britain (including the Count's mobile troops), a total for the fourth century British garrison of fewer than 8,000 men is implied here.

Although the question of whether or not soldiers' families were routinely to be found living within fort walls, thus producing units with fewer fighting men, is not likely to be resolved easily, it does not appear ever to have been a practice which would have been officially encouraged. An anonymous Byzantine military treatise of the mid-sixth century, for example, states that the '... men ... should not have their wives and children with them' except in conditions of peace and indeed recommends that families should deliberately be kept distant from troops.[29] It would be logical to expect, however, if chalets were indeed married quarters that their arrival in the fourth century should coincide with a compensating decline in vici, where traditionally soldiers' families are assumed to have lived. Although what evidence there is, based on pottery and coin finds, does indicate a decline in vicus life at many sites in the later third and fourth centuries (the Housesteads vicus, for example, was operating at a very reduced level by c. AD 300), the picture is far from conclusive and one obvious anomaly is Malton, which had a flourishing fourth century vicus, although Daniels has interpreted the substantial number of infant burials and possible existence of chalets there as pointing towards the transfer of families to within the fort walls.[30]

A comprehensive attack on the whole 'chalet' thesis has recently been launched by Paul Bidwell,[31] in which he concludes: 'The term 'chalet' now seems redundant, for it refers not to a separate building type, distinguished functionally by its series of detached blocks, but to a variant method of construction which has no necessary connection with the use of the building.'[32] Bidwell cites other examples, not used by Daniels, of the construction of detached buildings in forts well before Daniels' proposed Diocletianic dating for the introduction of the chalet scheme: a free-standing double barrack block built at Vindolanda in c. AD 235; several detached buildings at High Rochester of possibly a similar date; and detached blocks from Newstead constructed in the Antonine period. Bidwell concludes that detached blocks were not an innovation of the early fourth century but a much older reality in many instances and, in any case, were probably the result of being easier to produce in circumstances of poor carpentry skills or lack of suitable roof timbers[33] and not built as new-style married quarters. Intriguingly, he points out that Barrack XIV at Housesteads – arguably the starting point of the chalet concept – was later converted back from detached buildings to a continuous block. Daniels' argument for the chalet rebuilding as having been a planned development of the Diocletianic period is also rather uncomfortably dependent on assuming a long gap between the building (or re-building) of the earliest Saxon Shore forts and the construction of chalets for shrunken northern garrisons. In any case, although some units do appear to have been transferred directly from the northern frontier to the Saxon Shore, others were not. It is worth noting that, of Daniels' list

---

page 4). Wallsend's third and fouth century garrison regiment was *cohors III Lingonum* (**RIB** 1299-1301 and **Notitia**, Oc. 40, 33), a quingenary equitate unit.
[28] Nicholas Higham, **Rome, Britain and the Anglo-Saxons**, London, 1992, page 48.
[29] 'The Anonymous Byzantine Treatise On Strategy' in George T. Dennis (tr.), **Three Byzantine Military Treatises: Dumbarton Oaks Texts No. IX**, Washington, D.C., 1985 [pages 28/9]. Such condemnation all too typically of course reflected what was in fact happening by urging what should not take place.

[30] Roger Tomlin, **pers. comm.**, wonders if Malton was different because it was an industrial centre (the Crambeck potteries).
[31] Paul T. Bidwell, 'Later Roman barracks in Britain' in V. A. Maxfield & M.J. Dobson [edd.], **Roman Frontier Studies 1989**, Exeter, 1992, pages 9-15.
[32] Ibid., page 11.
[33] Peter Salway, **pers. comm.**, wonders if two centuries of deforestation had caused a shortage of large timber.

of eight probable chalet sites, four forts (Housesteads, Wallsend, Greatchesters and Chesters) all had garrison units recorded in the <u>Notitia</u> – and therefore presumably fourth century – which were identical to those of the third century.

Bidwell further draws attention to the calculation by Lindsay Allason-Jones[34] that Hadrian's Wall forts have actually produced more finds associated with women (trinkets, bracelets, beads and so on) dating from the second or early third centuries than from the fourth. Bidwell also wonders whether <u>vici</u> were ever primarily inhabited by soldiers' families or whether they served mostly as homes for merchants and craftsmen. He points out that no north British fort was more than two days' travel from a town and most were only one day (40 kilometres [25 miles]) away, and suggests that any decline in <u>vici</u> might have more to do with the growth and prosperity of towns than the transfer of familes to married quarters in forts. A shrinking market if units were smaller and the replacement of private suppliers by state factories might be additional factors contributing to the decline of <u>vici</u>.

Bidwell also argues persuasively that infant burials are not a strong argument for the development of married quarters in forts. They are rare (known only from four of the fifty or so forts occupied in the third and fourth centuries); not dated tidily from the post-Diocletianic period assumed to have seen the construction of chalets (one from Malton was from AD 260/80, and one from Little Chester first century); in some instances at least, were perhaps of a ritual nature; and, in any case, they may represent not families living in a military environment but rather the presence of civilians in a site temporarily abandoned (or partly abandoned) by the army.[35]

In conclusion, Bidwell argues that there are no convincing indications that barracks were converted to chalets for family units but there are indications of contubernia being reduced from the earlier eight-ten men to a lower five-six. Bidwell connects this with a reduction in century size from eighty men to sixty[36] and dates it to the mid-third century rather than later.[37] Apart from issues concerning construction, maintenance would have been greatly simplified by having smaller, separate accommodation units, as would the 'mothballing' or permanent closing down of parts of a fort. This apparent move away from a strict adherence to an official model towards a situation where practice more closely met real needs may also reflect a shift in the officer corps from the relative amateurs of the Principate to the professionals of the third century.[38]

One of the problems moreover with accepting Daniels' picture of a north British frontier with at least some forts with tiny garrisons is that it becomes difficult to see what function these troops would serve, other than as 'trip-wire' forces to buy time while field army reserves were deployed. In the third century the outpost forts of the Wall alone may have housed over 5,000 troops and their anticipatory and reconnaissance rôles would have been no less crucial once the outposts had been evacuated. The great superiority the Roman army possessed over its opponents, especially in the West, was its controlled mobility in the field but this function presumably devolved in the fourth century to the comitatensian forces behind the frontier as the strategy of having forward static units [limitanei] supported by mobile reserves [comitatenses] developed.

Nevertheless, the tiny units proposed by Daniels, and now receiving wide currency, would hardly allow for patrolling of any significance, let alone aggressive defence. Indeed these minuscule garrisons seem hardly capable of defending their forts. At Housesteads, eighty men were apparently expected to hold a rampart length of over 595 metres [651 yards]; while at Wallsend some fifty men were to defend 512 metres [560 yards] of rampart. Any commander could well have qualms at the prospect of withstanding a siege with each of his troops responsible for seven to nine metres [24 or 30 feet] of wall. As has been said, '... 4th century defences [on the

---

[34] **Women in Roman Britain**, London, 1989, pages 60-61.
[35] Bidwell, op. cit. (note 31), pages 12-14. Cf. also Sommer, op. cit. (note 26), page 52: 'As there is still no definite reason why civilians should have been admitted into still occupied forts at the end of the fourth century, the remains of civilians in forts should probably not be taken in general as evidence for periods of 'cohabitation' of civilians and soldiers, but as evidence for temporary abandonment of the forts under discussion.'

[36] Cf. E. Birley, 'Hadrian's Wall and its neighbourhood' in H. Schönberger (ed.), **Studien zu den Militärgrenzen Roms: Vorträge des 6. Internationalen Limeskongresses**, Köln, 1967, 6-14.
[37] Stephen Johnson [**The Roman Forts of the Saxon Shore**, London, 1976] suggests that most of the Saxon Shore forts were built in the period 276/285, a generation or so before Daniels' proposed timing of the appearance of chalets in the North.
[38] Peter Salway, **pers. comm.**

Wall] are essentially those built in the 2nd century. 2nd century forts were ... never designed to withstand siege, whereas most 4th century forts ... were.'[39]

Perhaps even chalet proponents need to consider whether such quarters need to be interpreted as housing only one fighting man (and his family). Daniels' Housesteads figures would allow a floor space of 4.6 x 8.2 metres [15 x 27 feet] per family group whereas a century of eighty men had shared a space of just 53 x 10 metres [175 x 32 feet] In other words, the chalet = married quarter thesis allows each soldier six times the room he had previously had; or it can be seen that each family unit required the same space that six adult soldiers (and their equipment) had been assigned before. If the 'chalets' are seen instead as new style blocks for smaller contubernia, then garrison sizes would still be reduced but far less dramatically: Housesteads to perhaps 400–480 men (50–60% of its second century establishment) and Wallsend to around 260–312 (43–52%).

Before leaving this issue of chalets, two other considerations should not be forgotten – both of which are little understood. In the first place, the whole chalet thesis – as propounded by Daniels and others – ignores the vital question of bachelor soldiers. There has been minimal examination of this subject but a small sample studied by Margaret Roxan[40] suggested that only about 50% of auxiliaries were married[41] and even if the minimum assumptions of the chalet thesis are to be accepted, then it follows that the resulting garrison sizes will need to be doubled to allow for bachelors and the problem of where they lived is left unresolved. Other estimates, however, have put the proportion of married soldiers much lower than this.[42]

Secondly, we also know that soldiers commonly had servants[43] – perhaps in very large numbers[44] – but there is no clear evidence as to where they were quartered, although they may of course have been housed in the vici. It may be that soldiers' servants were a more significant factor in cavalry units, where they acted as grooms and weapon-bearers.

Fort Sizes and Garrison Types

Several attempts have been made to see if a pattern of fort sizes and unit types can be distinguished: most of these have been inconclusive. Breeze and Dobson, for example, concluded[45] that an attempt by Ian Richmond[46] to classify British auxiliary forts according to their garrisons based on fort and barrack sizes 'cannot be accepted in [its] entirety.'[47] Mark Hassall has also looked at fort plans[48] but his studies have produced more anomalies than patterns, both in overall sizes and in internal arrangements. Examples can also be found of small forts which nevertheless seem to have had unexpectedly large garrisons: Kennedy and Riley[49] cite as examples Pen Llystyn which housed two cohorts in a site of just 1.8 hectares [4.5 acres] and Elginhaugh which squeezed a dozen barrack blocks and perhaps therefore just under a thousand troops into only 1.61 hectares [3.98 acres].

An even more obvious complication is that forts

---

[39] Jeremy Evans, 'Settlement and Society in North England in the Fourth Century' in P.R. Wilson, R.F.J. Jones and D.M. Evans [edd.], **Settlement and Society in the Roman North**, Bradford, 1984, page 43.
[40] 'Women on the Frontiers' in Maxfield and Dobson, op. cit. (note 31), pages 462–7.
[41] Roxan points out that this was very close to the (51%) ratio of married men in the British army in 1989. See also Brian Campbell, 'The Marriage of Soldiers under the Empire' in **JRS** 68, London, 1978, pages 153–166. Campbell commented: 'Perhaps a majority at any one time were bachelors' [page 155].
[42] Sommer, op. cit. (note 26), puts the proportion of married men much lower than 40%: he implies about 20%. Le Bohec, however (**The Imperial Roman Army**, London, 1994 [originally published as **L'Armée Romaine sous le Haut-Empire**, 1989], page 228) quotes substantial evidence for *legio III Augusta* in second century Numidia for a legionary level of well over 58% [unofficially] married soldiers. This higher proportion also presumably reflects the situation in a unit static in one station for a long time.
[43] **RIB** 1064, for example, is the tombstone of a twenty-year old Moor called Victor, freedman of one Numerianus a trooper of *ala I Asturum* from South Shields. Cf. Anthony Birley, **The People of Roman Britain**, London, 1979, page 148 for other British instances. For recently discovered examples, see now **Tab. Vindol.** II, 180, 28; II, 190, 26 etc.; and II, 301, quoted in Bowman (1994) as 6, 10 and 25.
[44] Cf. M.P. Speidel, 'The Soldiers' Servants' in Maxfield and Dobson, op. cit. (note 31), page 477 where he cites, for example, Tacitus's comment [**Histories** 2, 87] that Vitellius's army on its approach to Rome included even more camp followers [*calones*] than soldiers, of which there were 60,000. Camp followers were of course not necessarily all soldiers' servants, although a proportion of them may have been.
[45] David J. Breeze and Brian Dobson, 'Fort Types as a Guide to Garrisons: A Reconsideration' in Eric Birley, Brian Dobson and Michael Jarrett, **Roman Frontier Studies 1969**, Cardiff, 1974, pages 13–19.
[46] I.A. Richmond, 'Roman Britain and Roman Military Antiquities' in **Proceedings of the British Academy**, 1955, pages 297–315.
[47] Breeze and Dobson, op. cit. (note 45), page 18.
[48] Mark Hassall, 'The Internal Planning of Roman Auxiliary Forts' in Brian Hartley and John Wacher, **Rome and Her Northern Provinces**, Gloucester, 1983, pages 96–131.
[49] Op. cit. (note 1).

frequently saw changes of garrison with not just units but unit types being altered. On Hadrian's Wall, for example, the Notitia records alae where earlier there had been quingenary cohorts at Rudchester and Carrawburgh, while a quingenary rather than milliary cohort seems to have made up the garrison at Birdoswald, and at South Shields a quingenary ala had given way to a numerus. Whatever factors may have constrained the deployment of military units, the original garrison type of the posts concerned does not therefore appear to have been a consideration.

Archaeology and Literary References to Sieges

Although in the expansionist times of the Principate forts were no doubt regarded more as fortified bases for future advance (and therefore quite closely resembling many modern military sites) than as sites likely to be subject to siege, a fact that seems all too commonly ignored is that Roman forts were on occasions attacked and were sometimes captured, as were some of the cities garrisoned by military units. That this was a reality in the Late Empire too is reflected in part by the strong nature of forts of that period, typically having thick walls, massive corner towers and projecting interval towers: this is true even of small sites and the investment involved must clearly have related to a perception of a real danger of attack.[50] Some Norican examples of forts attacked in the fifth century are cited above.[51]

Examples of fortifications manned by surprisingly small garrisons may be drawn from many different periods and places. The massive 400-metre [1,312 feet] main curtain wall of Harlech Castle, for instance, was originally assigned (in 1284) a permanent garrison of a constable and '30 fencible men'; when the castle fell to Parliamentary forces on 15 March 1647, they captured just 52 defenders.[52] On the other hand, it took over 20,000 troops about two months to capture the Roman city of Constantinople during the 4th Crusade: one source put the defending Byzantine army at over 400,000 men.[53]

Is it possible then to seek evidence for a Roman doctrine on this issue of fort sizes and garrisons? There does in fact seem to be some indications that both officials and commentators understood the need for units to be able in extremis to defend their posts, and also the need to reduce fortified areas when appropriate.

Caesar, for example, describing the siege of Gergovia in 52 BC, refers to his inability to reduce the size of his larger camp when pulling out the bulk of the garrison: a camp originally held by six legions was left with just two.[54] The implication is that the reduction of a camp was routine and only the pressure of time had caused him on this occasion to leave the defences unaltered. It is interesting to note that this particular camp was apparently 36 hectares [ninety acres] in area: not unreasonably large by the standards of a permanent legionary fortress held by two legions.[55] Just as interestingly Caesar goes on to describe the difficulties faced by the camp defenders when attacked by the Gauls '... propter magnitudinem castrorum perpetuo esset isdem in vallo permanendum.'[56] Surely the normal practice must have been that some reserve was held back to relieve the defenders in the event of prolonged fighting.

Rather more than a century later Tacitus described the problems faced by under-manned forts at the beginning of the revolt of Civilis in AD 69. When Brinno, chief of the Cannenefates, attacked two forts usually identified as Valkenburg and Katwijk in a simultaneous land and maritime assault, he was successful because of the surprise nature of the attack and because the garrisons '... would not have been strong enough to hold out [even] if they had [expected attack] ...'[57]

Tacitus describes how, immediately afterwards, the cohort prefects in command destroyed the frontier forts which were about to be attacked '... because they could not be defended ...' due to the fact that '... Vitellius had withdrawn the bulk

---

[50] Cf. Dionysias in Egypt, Veriaraca and Anabatha in Phoenicia, Resafa in Syria and the Saxon Shore forts in Britain.
[51] See Chapter 3, page 30.
[52] Arnold Taylor, **Harlech Castle**, Cardiff, 1988, pages 6 and 10.
[53] Geoffroy de Villehardouin, **Conquest of Constantinople**, chapter 12. Villehardouin put the original Crusader army, three years earlier, at some 33,500 men. The Byzantine annalist, Niketas Choniates [**O City of Byzantium**, chapter 539] gives a very similar figure – 31,000. Villehardouin's figure for the Byzantine defenders seems a typical example of mediaeval exaggeration; in the siege of 1453, the city was defended by some 7,000 men.
[54] Caesar, **De bello Gallico**, 7, 40.
[55] Cf. Keppie, op. cit. (note 21), page 88. The double legionary fortress at Vetera covered about 56 hectares [138 acres]: cf. Keppie, op. cit., fig. 52, page 195. Caesar's camp was of course a temporary campaigning base. There are still doubts however whether Gergovie really is Caesar's Gergovia.
[56] Ibid., 7, 41. Cf. Keppie, op. cit. (note 21), page 88.
[57] Tacitus, **Histories**, 4, 16.

of [their] effectives ....'[58] It is clear that Tacitus was taking it as self-evident that fort garrisons could not be indefinitely weakened and still be able to man their defences successfully.

Then, when Civilis laid siege to Vetera (Xanten), Tacitus wrote: 'The attacking force was encouraged by the length of the rampart, which, although designed for two legions [sc. V and XV], was in fact defended by barely 5,000 armed men.'[59] Archaeology has revealed that Vetera I, a Neronian stone rebuilt double fortress of the late 50s, was indeed about twice the size of a standard fortress: it covered some 56 hectares [138 acres] with ramparts measuring 902 x 621 metres [2,959 x 2,037 feet].[60] Evidently the reduction of the intended garrison by a factor of 50% was expected to cause problems for the defenders.

Although these examples date from the late Republic and early Empire, they represent at least unexceptionable plausibility and perhaps even a military doctrine reflecting obvious common sense. A similar attitude is also reflected in the comment from Vegetius quoted above[61] in which he clearly argues that fort sizes ought to be appropriate to the garrison in question.

Towns

A final complication which needs to be borne in mind when considering the whole issue of the relationship between fort size and unit size is that a substantial proportion of Late Army units were, of course, not stationed in forts at all but were mobile formations, billetted in towns, often in specific districts, when not on campaign; they were entitled to one-third of the available accommodation, and this stipulation proved no more popular than the compulsory stationing of troops among civilians has usually been. Mobile formations generally had no fixed bases and are listed as such in the Notitia; there is, for example, no way of ascertaining where the nine regiments assigned to the regional field army of the comes Britanniae were at any time stationed. There is of course therefore no archaeological basis for speculating on the size of such units.

In addition, many Late Army frontier units, or at least garrisons classified as limitanei, were also urban-based. MacMullen[62] lists a number of such garrison towns, which were mostly frontier towns or legionary fortresses which had acquired civilian populations. They included Tiaret in Mauretania Caesariensis; Tours; Umm-Idj-Djimal in southern Syria; Palmyra (modern Tadmor near Homs) in Syria [where the legion I Illyricorum was probably stationed in the 8-hectare Castra Diocletiana]; Chersonesus; Castra Regina (modern Regensburg) in Germany [base of elements of the legion III Italica]; Vindonissa (modern Windisch) in Switzerland; Argentorate (modern Strasbourg); Damascus; and Magnesia.

---

[58] Ibid..
[59] Op. cit., 4, 23.
[60] Cf. Keppie, op. cit. (note 21), pages 194-5.
[61] Chapter 3, note 65.

[62] Ramsay MacMullen, **Soldier and Civilian in the Later Roman Empire,** Cambridge, Mass., 1963.

CHAPTER 6
CONCLUSIONS

When we turn to consider what conclusions about unit sizes can be drawn from the evidence cited above, it is necessary to begin by stressing the uncertainty present even for the simpler and better documented situation of the Principate. Although the margin of doubt is not unduly large, it is not insignificant, and is more of a problem for some unit types than others. We can assert with reasonable confidence for example, that the legions of the Early Empire had an official establishment in the region of 5,100–5,200 men, without forgetting that such an establishment is nowhere stated in our sources.

The division of the auxiliary units into six types with a large overall majority each containing a nominal 500 troops (quingenary)[1] and a substantial minority of nominally double that strength (milliary) does suggest intended establishments but we only need to recall that legionary centuries ('units of 100') illogically but unarguably contained eighty men each to appreciate that the process of theory being overtaken by reality all too often rendered the implications of such terminology less than meaningful.[2] If we consider the unit type descriptors for the various auxiliary formations ('quingenary peditate cohort', 'milliary ala', etc.) in conjunction with the limited literary evidence available (from Arrian and especially Vegetius), various quantities of possible establishments with appropriate levels of certainty emerge. Quingenary peditate cohorts almost definitely contained 480 men each in theory; milliary peditate cohorts very probably had 800 men each; quingenary alae were almost certainly in the region of 512–528 strong; and milliary alae were more likely to have had about 760–800 men than anything higher. The part-mounted (equitate) units present greater difficulties but the outside range of possibilities is no wider than 480–608 for quingenary units and 820–1,100 for milliary regiments; removing the more speculative suggestions and placing more faith in the statements of Vegetius would narrow the possibilities to 600–608 and 1,000–1,056 respectively.[3]

The small amount of documentary evidence that survives for the Principate provides some limited support for certain elements of the pattern suggested above.[4] The single document that appears to be a record of a milliary peditate cohort puts that unit at about 94% of the establishment of 800 proposed above, while for the only unit type for which any substantial documentation survives – the quingenary equitate cohort – it seems difficult to dispute a structure of six centuries and four turmae with an overall establishment of about 600 men. It is significant that the three records for quingenary equitate cohorts available show such units at 91%, 84% and 76–81% of the theoretical 600 which has been proposed as the most likely establishment, even though the documents are from different parts of the Empire and cover a century or so. Without ignoring the limited and random nature of the surviving evidence or the problems created by the peculiar unit size and structure recorded in the files of XX Palmyrenorum, it is nevertheless encouraging that for the one area where any significant quantity of documentation exists, it reinforces rather than weakens the literary evidence.

Although there is no evidence that the legions raised by Marcus Aurelius and Septimius Severus were smaller than the 5,000-strong units of the Early Principate, the process of the emergence of a field army can be traced back at least as far as those reigns. By the mid-third century a substantial reserve force had been formed, partly by the raising of new units but also through detaching elements from units already in existence. The most significant point thereafter was the reign of Diocletian, when the army was substantially increased in overall numbers and many new units were established. The quantity of legions deployed went up during that reign by at least 50% and more probably by about 100%: this was between six and eleven times more than the largest previous number of legions raised at any one time. Although some of the other new, non-legionary

---

[1] 88% of second century units were quingenary – about 339 out of 387 according to Dr Brian Dobson, 'The Empire' in **Warfare in the Ancient World**, edited by General Sir John Hackett, London, 1989, pages 192–221.
[2] In the modern Royal Air Force, Flight Lieutenants rarely command flights, Squadron Leaders are invariably too junior to command squadrons, Wing Commanders do not normally command wings and the organisational unit 'Group' no longer exists for Group Captains to command.
[3] It is worth noting that the enormous range of possible sizes and structures for milliary equitate cohorts relates to regiments of which fewer than two dozen examples existed.
[4] No document from any period records the details of an entire legion.

Diocletianic units were formed by dividing existing ones or taking detachments from them, the recruiting of at least some troops for these units must have been needed and this fact, together with the creation of many new legions, is perhaps the single, strongest argument that such formations must have been smaller than their equivalents from the Principate. Although this has no necessary implication for the pre-existing units – and the possibility of the co-existence of two different establishments, for example for legions, should be considered – it makes an overwhelming case for the new, Diocletianic legions being 1,000–2,000–strong rather than any larger. As well as the insuperable problems of recruitment that would otherwise have had to be faced, the consequences for the Imperial Treasury of such a sudden and enormous increase in the military pay bill are unthinkable.[5]

The process of the growth of the central reserve forces continued apace under Constantine and by the end of the fourth century well over 300 mobile units existed. Although these forces were made up of new-style units – cavalry vexillationes, infantry legiones, auxilia and legiones pseudocomitatenses – rather than old-style cohortes and alae, it is very difficult to assign them even quingenary strengths as a generality: using such a crude measure, however, the mobile armies would have totalled well over 150,000 men.[6] Although not a completely incredible figure, a rather lower one would fit more comfortably with the events of the Late Empire and particularly with the size of expeditionary forces that are reported. There seems little doubt in any case that, for instance, the field army 'legions' must have borne little resemblance in terms of size (and presumably structure) to their namesakes of the Principate: mobile legions 5,000-strong would have produced a total for these units alone of a quite incredible half a million men.[7]

The literary evidence that can be brought to bear on this subject is limited but there are some references – both direct and implicit – to small units. Ammianus's account of the garrison of Amida in AD 359, where he details the units and calculates the number of the besieged, argues strongly for relatively small legions (of perhaps one or two thousand men). The same implication for field army regiments can be drawn from the combination of Claudian's order of battle for the North African expedition of AD 398 and Orosius's statement about the size of that force. It is also possible to infer small field army units from references by Zosimus to events in AD 409 and 410 but, in these instances, it is far from clear what type of units are being cited. And finally, a clear reference to a very small force of Late Roman soldiers in Libya is found in Synesius's description of a victory won by just forty men. What needs to be remembered in this case however is that it is not known whether these Hunnish troops were regulars or whether the force described was an actual unit per se.

It is difficult to claim that this is an impressively large body of evidence and there are moreover contradictory references. Libanius, the Historia Augusta, Vegetius, Zosimus and John Lydus are all sources from the fourth-sixth centuries referring to army units – legions, alae and cohorts – at or near the sizes traditionally assumed for the Early Empire. Although it is usual to dismiss these writers as unreliable or backward-looking or both, caution might suggest some hesitation before rejecting them all out of hand. It is true that few of these writers had military experience and that the focus of interest for Vegetius and John Lydus was very much antiquarian but, on the other hand, the writers cited in defence of the case for small units include a poet and an academic cleric. The only real military expert at all among the writers of the Late Empire was Ammianus and the evidence he provides is far from unambiguous. It does, for example, include a reference to what are perhaps alae, which he implies had totals of 350 men. Such a figure is obviously smaller than the norm assumed for the Principate (68% of 512) but, if it is not to be explained by combat attrition, may reflect a new, lower establishment. Contradictions in our literary sources may mean that some evidence has to be rejected as inaccurate but it could also suggest a more complex situation accurately described: we are not however able to quantify the proportions of small units and larger ones – although the former were presumably a significant majority. With the honorable exception of Ammianus, none of the authors referred to here were familiar with army life and organisation, and even Ammianus adhered to the literary conventions of the classical historians who had avoided employing technical terms. A modern student would not instinctively turn to a bishop,

---

[5] Even the lower level of new units would have meant a very large increase in expenditure (and incidentally of officers).
[6] 500 x 325 = 162,500.
[7] Roger Tomlin, 'The Mobile Army' in Peter Connolly (ed.) **Greece and Rome at War**, London, 1981, page 254 estimates some 93 mobile legions. 93 x 5,000 = 465,000.

a poet laureate, a civil servant or a university professor of rhetoric if seeking details of military unit sizes but that is in effect what the student of the Late Roman Army is obliged to do.

Perhaps the most influential source of all for the question of unit sizes in the Late Roman Army is the Panopolis papyri, despite the irony that nowhere do they explicitly provide such details. Jones's interpretation of the documents produced legionary vexillations of between about 850 and 2,000 men, a cohort at about the strength[8] of the assumed Principate norm of 480 and alae at 69/72% and 42% of the assumed norm of 512. Duncan-Jones's re-interpretation halved the vexillation figures and reduced the auxiliary units to a cohort at 34% of norm, and alae at 22% and 4% of norm. That last figure (an ala with just 21½ soldiers at two sites) is perhaps the most interesting and the most overlooked of all Duncan-Jones's calculations. Although his estimate of ala I Hiberorum having 116/118 troopers has achieved wide acceptance as a typical Late Empire cavalry regiment size, there is no intrinsic reason why it should be any more typical than Duncan-Jones's other ala estimate – that II Herculia Dromedariorum contained fewer than two dozen men. It is difficult to avoid concluding that an evidently absurd result has been rejected in favour of one less so,[9] whereas a greater scepticism about the whole structure of calculation involved could be advised. Even Jones's earlier and higher estimates had included significant reductions in the cavalry units compared with the unit sizes assumed for earlier. The cavalry would of course have been more difficult to train and more expensive to maintain, so that the Late Roman Army may have experienced greater difficulties in keeping mounted units up to establishment compared with the infantry.[10] In any case, even if the whole of Duncan-Jones's thesis about the Panopolis documents is to be accepted as correct, that relates only to one particular place and time without any necessary Empire-wide implications. Interestingly, with the exception of Synesius (who, it should be stressed again, may not have been referring to a unit), none of the literary sources refer to units as small as the cohorts and alae suggested by Duncan-Jones.

The survival of a list of Late Army units – even if the Notitia is probably not an official order of battle – is extremely fortunate and, whatever mistakes the list contains, it should allow at least the establishment of certain unit size maxima. Nearly 200 legions, for instance, cannot all have numbered 5,000 men each; very possibly none of them were of anything like that size.[11] Over 120 groups of equites similarly must have included many very small units. There is of course no reason to insist on supposing that all units with the same type name had identical sizes or structures, either in theory or in practice. Various attempts have been made to turn the Notitia lists into army sizes and to extrapolate unit sizes from that but the degree of uncertainty involved in such exercises is high. Overall Late Army sizes from as low as a quarter of a million men or so up to well over half a million have been calculated; the field army size suggestions cited above[12] range between about 130,000 and about 250,000. On the whole, the very small quantity of evidence in the Notitia explicitly referring to units of particular sizes (such as 'centenaria' and 'milliaria') is probably best disregarded, as reflecting a historical rather than a current reality.

Archaeology has produced some evidence for small forts from the Late Empire and, where these sites can be linked to known units with traditional titles, they suggest a strong assumption that such units must have been smaller than their counterparts from the first and second centuries. Small forts have been identified in the East and on the Rhine-Danube frontier; although the widespread practice of splitting units between different posts may be an additional factor involved, some of the forts were extremely tiny and can only have housed very weak garrisons. The re-development of North British barracks into 'chalets' to serve as married quarters, on the other hand, probably still needs to be seen as an unproven thesis. Garrison units may indeed have been run down but not necessarily by the drastic amounts sometimes suggested. It should also be noted that several Roman writers, from the Republic to the Late Empire, demonstrate that the need

---

[8] Between 94 and 109%.
[9] A similar point could be made about legionary vexillations. Duncan-Jones's smallest calculation is for a detachment (from the legion II Traiana) of just over 77 men but this has not usually been taken to represent a norm.
[10] Although of course the *pridiana* tend to suggest the reverse: that cavalry were the priority arm and that more effort was made to keep them up to strength compared with the infantry.

[11] Most detailed calculations (such as those of Jones and Várady) in fact allow for two establishments for legions with a larger one for limitanean units. The Notitia lists include only 41 such 'frontier' legions.
[12] See above page 43.

for garrisons to be appropriate to the size of their forts was well understood and the dangers to posts held by understrength units were appreciated.

The remarkable survival over many centuries of some units of the Roman Army should not lead to the assumption that these units necessarily remained unchanged in terms of size and structure. We do know that new titles for unit commanders and a new hierarchy of ranks for at least some regiments had developed by the late fourth century but it is not clear how widely the latter applied nor what this implied for unit sizes. The internal re-organisation of units may suggest a logical relationship with numbers of troops in units but this cannot yet be demonstrated for certain. The limited evidence there is on this subject is ambiguous: legio II Herculia, for example, was a Diocletianic creation with a typically Late Empire fortress only about one seventh the size of an average legionary base of the Principate but it seems to have comprised a full complement of ten cohorts. One difficulty in assuming a small legion but with a traditional structure is to extrapolate from this what might have been the sub-unit sizes: if cohorts were near to century-size, did they in turn contain 'centuries' and, if so, how many men did they include?[13]

Although we would do well to beware the tendency of observers of most periods to bemoan the failings of the current time and to look back to a probably mythical golden age,[14] there is an inescapable consciousness of decline among certain writers of the Late Empire and this extends to their attitude towards the Imperial army. Before his detailed description of the 'ancient legion', Vegetius[15] describes how the title survived into his own time but was applied to units depleted by the effects of neglect, corruption and lack of recruiting. Agathias, writing over a century and a half later, writes movingly of 'The Roman armies ... [which] had dwindled to a fraction of what they had been and were no longer adequate to the requirements of a vast empire.'[16] He claimed that the army had shrunk to less than a quarter of its authorised establishment and was unable to put up an effective defence against the invasion of the Cotrigurs in AD 559: 'There was nothing to stop them, no sentries, no engines of defence, nobody to man them. There was not even the sound of a dog barking, as would at least have been the case with a pig-sty or a sheep-cot.'[17]

One factor of real decline that may lie behind the image of decline is reflected by a number of references to the practice of units containing 'ghost' soldiers. Libanius, for example, wrote that the dead were 'kept alive' so that their rations could still be drawn.[18] His contemporary and fellow orator, Themistius, referred to a similar practice in an oration delivered early in AD 370: Valens, he claimed, had restored Danubian forts 'whose garrisons were ... fraudulent.'[19] Themistius made it clear that the obvious purpose of keeping 'ghost' soldiers was to be able to continue to claim their pay; he made the same point about fraudulently enrolled soldiers in another oration.[20] The practice of retaining on the muster rolls dead soldiers was recorded again during Justinian's reign by Procopius, who claimed it was the official policy of the Treasury agents called Logothetes. In this instance, it is far from clear what the point of having 'ghost' soldiers was but Procopius stressed its effect of keeping the army under-strength[21]. Something like official conniving at or a despairing acceptance of desertion is reflected in the edict of AD 413,

---

[13] Assuming the retention of a classical establishment of 1 legion = 10 cohorts and 1 cohort = 6 centuries (and ignoring any complications of the 1st Cohort), then a legion of 1,000 men would have contained cohorts of 100 and centuries of 17. A legion only one-seventh the size of an Early Empire legion (about 700 men) would, on the same basis, have contained cohorts of 70 and centuries of 12. These are not easy figures to credit but it has been suggested [Peter Salway, **pers. comm.**] that Diocletian himself may have consciously retained the existing legionary structure within the new small legions to allow for the rapid absorption of recruits in time of crisis; such an intention need not imply that any such expansion ever took place.
[14] Cf. Horace, Ars Poetica: 'laudatur temporis acti se puero.'
[15] Vegetius, Epitoma rei militaris, 2, 3.
[16] Agathias, The Histories, Book 5, 13, 7. Translation from the edition by Joseph D. Frendo, Corpus Fontium Historiae Byzantinae Volume IIA, Berlin, 1975, page 148.
[17] Ibid., Book 5, 13, 6.
[18] Libanius, Oration 47, 31. Examples can be found quite easily of the spurious nature of paper strengths from the better documented 20th Century. For example, at the end of April 1945 (within a week of the end of hostilities) the German Army still fielded a theoretical total in excess of 240 divisions on the Eastern, Western and Italian fronts. In reality the vast majority of these units contained only a small fraction even of the reduced establishments of that period, and many had virtually no combat value at all.
[19] Themistius, Oration 10 (On the Peace of Valens), 136 b.
[20] Themistius, Oration 8, 116.
[21] Procopius, Anecdota, 24, 5-6. Peter Salway [**pers. comm.**] suggests that the existence of the 'ghosts' soldiers may have been a cunning bureaucratic method of increasing military pay and allowances without setting a precedent.

which prescribed nothing more severe than demotion for a year's absence without leave, and allowed deserters to remain on the 'official register' until a period of four years absence had elapsed![22] The custom of military units including non-existent personnel, either by retaining on the records the deceased or by other means, is known from many other periods of history. It was not always an unofficial or corrupt practice: a British army regiment of Foot was assigned a theoretical strength of 423 privates in 1763 but this figure included about twenty 'contingent men': these were ... 'non-existent soldiers whose pay the companies drew to cover hospital expenses, repairs to weapons and accoutrements, funerals, and similar expenses ....'[23]

If it can be considered as at least possible that the practice of including non-existent soldiers was widespread, then the confidence that can be placed in unit size estimates based even on surviving documentation will not be particularly high. The three instances cited above date from the fourth and sixth centuries but it can be by no means certain that the lack of evidence relating to earlier periods indicates that 'ghost' soldiers did not exist then. It may of course partially help to explain the military setbacks of the Late Empire if allowance has to be made for units being in actuality weaker than the theoretical establishments that have been deduced from, for example, the Notitia lists. The Iberian regional field army of the comes Hispaniae, for example, which was probably formed as an emergency force in the period 407–409, counted 16 regiments[24] – a force which might have been expected to number 8,000–16,000 men – but appears to have played little or no part in resisting the invasion of the Vandals, Suebi and Alans in the autumn of 409; they may however have been the troops who mutinied against Gerontius. When the Western government launched a campaign of reconquest in Spain in the period 416–418, they employed the Visigothic forces of Vallia and it seems an inescapable implication that the Count of Spain's army no longer existed. Similarly weak or virtually non-existent field armies can be inferred from the events during Alaric's invasion of Greece in 394/5 which in theory should have been defended by 26 field army regiments,[25] from the need to defend the Rhine frontier in 406 with Frankish federates and from the rapid Vandal conquest of North Africa in the 420s. Even Stilicho seems to have had available only one truly effective field army – that of Italy. Between a half and two-thirds of the entire field army strength had probably been lost in the late fourth and early fifth centuries: these losses were partly made good but only by stripping the frontier of <u>limitanei</u>, especially in Gaul.

There is a substantial body of evidence that by the fourth century a clear division existed in terms of quality and prestige between the limitanean and comitatensian troops, even if those technical terms were not in use until later. This was expressed in clear legal terms: for example, field army troops were allowed a more favourable tax status and they were expected to meet more stringent physical standards.[26] The poor quality of the <u>limitanei</u> and their eventual decline to a type of peasant militia is still cited as axiomatic by some authorities but the evidence suggests a more complex reality. Jones[27] cited examples of soldiers who appear also to have been farmers, traders, bakers, basket weavers and boatmen. There is however an increasing body of evidence – especially the Vindolanda tablets – which is providing a picture of a well-developed unofficial economy among the officers and men on the northern frontier of first and early second century Britain;[28] there is no suggestion however that the 9th Batavians or the 1st Tungrians were in any sense part-time soldiers or made inefficient by their trading and lending.

It is often forgotten that Imperial troops were specifically forbidden to hold land in the province in which they were serving[29] and,

---

[22] **CTh** 7, 18, 16.
[23] John R. Elting, **The Battle of Bunker's Hill**, Monmouth Beach, New Jersey, 1975, page 52 quoting War Office 1/980 f 265. A modern instance is cited in **The Guardian** of 8th August 1994 where an article on Cambodia refers to an 'estimated 30,000 to 40,000 'phantom' soldiers on the army payroll' as a money-raising scheme for senior officers.
[24] All incidentally infantry.

[25] Cf. J.H.W.G. Liebeschuetz, **Barbarians and Bishops: Army, Church and State in the Age of Arcadius and Chrysostom**, Oxford, 1990.
[26] Cf. Benjamin Isaac, 'The Meaning of The Terms Limes and Limitanei' in **J.R.S.**, 78, London, 1988, pages 141 (citing **CTh** 7, 20, 4) and 142 (citing **CTh** 7, 22, 8 and 13, 7, 3).
[27] A.H.M. Jones, **The Decline of the Ancient World**, London, 1966, pages 227–8.
[28] Cf. Alan K. Bowman, **Life and Letters on the Roman Frontier**, London, 1994, 20, pages 125–6 (= **Tab. Vindol**. 2, 225). There are other examples of business deals recorded in the Vindolanda tablets but this item is one that clearly involved two serving soldiers (a prefect and a centurion).
[29] **Digest** 49, 16, 13 (Aemilius Macer) cited in C. Sebastian Sommer **The Military Vici in Roman Britain: Aspects of their Origins, their Locations and**

although this prohibition was eventually lifted, the first record of limitanei officially working the land occurs as late as AD 443.[30] This does not of course imply any imposition of an hereditary status on these troops nor that cultivating their own land '... seriously affected their professional duties.'[31] Limitanean units formed the garrison which successfully defended Amida against the Persians in AD 359; Julian included limitanei in his Persian expedition four years later; and limitanei were of sufficient quality to be transferred to the comitatenses on more than one occasion. Even as late as the mid-sixth century, Belisarius was able to deploy limitanei from Phoenicia-Libanensis against the Persians in Mesopotamia.

One aspect of the Late Roman Army that is still a matter of controversy is the extent to which it was 'barbarianised'. Some contemporary observers strongly criticised official policy of recruiting barbarians: Vegetius was keen to purge the army of non-Romans[32] and Synesius urged their removal from the Eastern field army in AD 399: 'We must ... get used to winning our own victories, not putting up with partners but dismissing the barbarian from every rank and post.'[33] Synesius of course later changed his mind and praised the Huns who fought with him in north Africa but such purges did take place on occasions, sometimes with great violence: in 408, for instance, the families of 30,000 Gothic federates were massacred.[34]

It has been fairly remarked that the use of allied troops must have reflected the weakness of the regular forces: otherwise there '... could hardly have been much need to resort to barbarian federates ....'[35] This dependency is not at all easy to quantify however. Liebeschuetz has argued on a number of occasions[36] that this

barbarian element of the Late Roman Army was highly significant and '... by 450 the bulk of the field army ... in the West consisted of federates.'[37] Recently it has been suggested that the rôle of barbarians in the fourth and fifth centuries has been overstated and the proportion of them was probably no higher than about 25%.[38]

Whatever may have been the truth about this issue, the forces of the Western Empire – limitanei and mobile forces – gradually but largely disappeared during the course of the fifth century. Some elements of the army in Britain may have survived beyond the break with the central government in 409–410 but there is little certainty about this. The north African army must have disappeared by the final Vandal conquest of the 450s; the Spanish army could have lasted little longer. Eugippius has left a vivid picture of the decline of the garrison of Noricum. Julius Nepos may have continued to command the remnants of the army of Illyricum until his death in 480. The end of the large army of Italy is an even more mysterious process. The last elements of the army of Gaul are usually thought to have been defeated by Clovis in 486 but it has been suggested that some final traces of late Roman military organisation survived under Merovingian control into the next century.[39]

Layout, Administration, Function and End, BAR British Series 129, Oxford, 1984.
[30] NTh 24, 1, 4 = CJ 1, 60, 3 (12 September AD 443) cited in Isaac, op. cit. (note 26), page 145.
[31] Isaac, op. cit., (note 26), page 146. He points out that many of the most effective armies of the modern world contain substantial militia elements: he could have cited the armies of Israel, Sweden and Switzerland.
[32] Cf. especially 1, 28 and 3, 1.
[33] Synesius, **De Regno**, [19] 23B = 1092C-1093A.
[34] Zosimus, **Nea Historia**, 5, 35, 5–6.
[35] Averil Cameron, **The Later Roman Empire AD 284-430**, London, 1993, page 147.
[36] J.H.G.W. Liebeschuetz, 'Generals, Federates and Bucellarii in Roman Armies Around AD 400' in Philip Freeman and David Kennedy [edd.], **The Defence of the Roman and Byzantine East: Proceedings of a Colloquium held at the University of Sheffield in April 1986**, BAR International Series 297, Oxford, 1986, pages 463-474, reprinted in **From Diocletian to the Arab Conquest: Change in the Late Roman Empire**,

Aldershot, 1990 (19); J.H.W.G. Liebeschuetz, **Barbarians and Bishops: Army, Church and State in the Age of Arcadius and Chrysostom**, Oxford, 1990; and Wolfgang Liebeschuetz, 'The end of the Roman army in the western empire' in John Rich and Graham Shipley [edd.], **War and Society in the Roman World**, Leicester-Nottingham Studies in Ancient Society Volume 5, London, 1993, pages 265-276.
[37] Liebeschuetz, 1993, page 273.
[38] Hugh Elton, **Aspects of Defence in Roman Europe AD 350-500** [unpublished D.Phil. thesis], Oxford, 1990, cited in Liebeschuetz, 1993, page 266. The sample involved however is very small.
[39] B.S. Bachrach, **Merovingian Military Organization 481-751**, Minneapolis, 1972, pages 33-4, cited in Liebeschuetz, 1993, page 273, note 2. It also needs to be remembered that the Roman Army performed a whole series of non-military functions. They acted in effect as a sort of 'highway patrol'. The army had had for a long time a 'civil service' function: they were used, for example, to collect taxes. They served as the empire's customs service. They had a significant function as very often the only police force available for dealing with criminal activity. In many provinces they had a crucial rôle as an internal security arm: a turbulent region like Judaea, although it had no external frontier, housed a very large garrison including two legions and several thousand auxiliaries in order to suppress banditry and rebellion. The army continued to play a similar rôle in the Late Empire: in AD 387, for instance, troops from the field army command of the *comes Orientis* were deployed to put down the 'riot of the statues' in Antioch. The increased need for the police function of the army may

help to explain its increasing fragmentation: '... the need to use the troops for internal security made it sensible to disperse them into smaller units' (Averil Cameron, op. cit. [note 35], page 114). It is difficult to avoid the inference that, as the quantity and probably the quality of troops available to the government declined – especially in the West – so the breakdown of those civil functions of the armed forces contributed to the weakening of the whole Imperial structure. On the question of the army's non–military rôle, see especially Averil Cameron, op. cit. (note 35) and David Kennedy and Derrick Riley, **Rome's Desert Frontier: From the Air**, London, 1990.

AFTERWORD

It can be seen then that the evidence for unit sizes in the Late Roman Army is limited in quantity and less than conclusive in nature. The surviving literary material is restricted in quantity and contradictory in detail; the documentary evidence is not extensive and, although some of it can be interpreted as showing small unit numbers, it is difficult to quantify this reduction with certainty or safely to generalize from it; and, although there is archaeological evidence for both reduced and newly built small forts, some of the extrapolations calculated for garrison numbers are not soundly based. An assumption that many fourth and early fifth century units contained numbers of troops much fewer than their equivalents during the Principate seems nevertheless inescapable, if only because of the very much larger number of, for instance, legions that formed part of the Imperial Order of Battle from the last years of the third century. Beyond that, however, little in the way of certainties exists – whether in terms of the size of Late Army units or of the possibility that different establishments co-existed. Caution is therefore essential before further implications are explored.

The discovery of further documentary evidence relating to the subject is of course quite possible and the survival of a range of organic materials at Vindolanda suggests that the search for such materials need not be confined to traditionally productive areas such as Egypt. Archaeological work is even more likely to add to the evidence available on this subject: the kind of detailed excavations undertaken at El-Lejjun, for example, could usefully be carried out at other small Eastern sites as a basis for estimating the sizes of garrisons recorded by documentary or epigraphic sources, while there is also the possibility of studying changes in use of internal fort space. Data might, for instance, be acquired through a programme of geophysical survey within Later Roman forts with computer analysis of spatial patterns. An examination of fort cemeteries with the possible use of DNA analysis might shed light on matters relating to the proportion of married soldiers and family accommodation, while further study of numismatic evidence might help to indicate fluctuations in wage totals and therefore unit sizes.

This thesis has been concerned primarily with an examination of the evidence available at the moment for the question of Late Roman Army unit sizes. It has also considered and analysed earlier interpretation of this evidence and of generalisations derived from such interpretations. It is hoped that certain common misconceptions will have been exposed and perhaps undermined. The way should also have been opened up for others – particularly those working with different techniques – further to examine the issue.

BIBLIOGRAPHY

Agathias, *The Histories*.
Leslie Alcock, *Arthur's Britain*, London, 1971.
Géza Alföldy, *Noricum*, [tr. Anthony Birley], London and Boston, 1974.
Lindsay Allason-Jones, *Women in Roman Britain*, London, 1989.
Ammianus Marcellinus, *Histories*.
Anglo-Saxon Chronicle.
L'Année Epigraphique, Paris, 1888–.
S. Archer, 'Late Roman Gold and Silver Coin Hoards in Britain: A Gazetteer' in *The End of Roman Britain* BAR British Series 71, Oxford, 1979, pages 29–64.
Arrian, *Tactica*.
Augustine, *City of God*.
N.J.E. Austin, *Ammianus on Warfare: An Investigation into Ammianus' Military Knowledge*, Collection Latomus Volume 165, Brussels, 1979.
B.S. Bachrach, *Merovingian Military Organization 481–751*, Minneapolis, 1972.
Philip Bartholomew, 'Fourth-Century Saxons' in *Britannia* 15, London, 1984, pages 169–185.
Bede, *Historia Ecclesiastica*.
H.I. Bell, V. Martin, E.G. Turner and D. van Berchem [edd.], *The Abinnaeus Archive: Papers of a Roman Officer in the Reign of Constantius II*, Oxford, 1962.
Berliner griechische Urkunden (Agyptische Urkunden aus den königlichen Museen zu Berlin), Berlin, 1895–.
Martin Biddle, *Fourth Century Fables*, the Fourth Graham Webster Lecture [unpublished], given at the University of Birmingham, 1987.
Paul T. Bidwell, 'Later Roman Barracks in Britain' in V. A. Maxfield & M.J. Dobson [edd.], *Roman Frontier Studies 1989*, Exeter, 1992, pages 9–15.
Paul T. Bidwell, *The Roman Fort of Vindolanda: at Chesterholm, Northumberland*, Historic Buildings and Monuments Commission for England Archaeological Report No. 1, London, 1985.
Paul Bidwell and David Speak, 'South Shields' in *Current Archaeology*, 116 (August 1989), pages 283–287.
A.R. Birley, 'The Economic Effects of Roman Frontier Policy' in Anthony King and Martin Henig [edd.], *The Roman West in the Third Century: Contributions from Archaeology and History*, BAR International Series 109 (i), Oxford, 1981, pages 39–53.
Anthony R. Birley, *The Fasti of Roman Britain*, Oxford, 1981.
Anthony Birley, *The People of Roman Britain*, London, 1979.
A. R. Birley, 'Vindolanda: new writing tablets 1986–89' in V. A. Maxfield & M.J. Dobson [edd.], *Roman Frontier Studies 1989*, Exeter, 1992, pages 16 ff..
Eric Birley, 'Alae and Cohortes Milliariae' in *Corolla memoriae Erich Swoboda Dedicata*, Römische Forschungen in Niederösterreich V, 1966, pages 54–67.
E Birley, 'Hadrian's Wall and its neighbourhood' in H. Schönberger (ed.), *Studien zu den Militärgrenzen Roms: Vorträge des 6. Internationalen Limeskongresses*, Köln, 1967, 6–14.
Eric Birley, 'Local Militias in the Roman Empire' in *Bonner Historia-Augusta-Colloquium 1972/1974*, Bonn, 1976, pages 65–73, reprinted in *Mavors 4, Roman Army Researches Volume 4*, Amsterdam, 1988, pages 387–394.
Eric Birley, 'Septimius Severus and the Roman Army' in *Epigraphische Studien* 8 (1969), pages 63–82, reprinted in M.P. Speidel (ed.), *The Roman Army: Papers 1929–1986 = Mavors: Roman Army Researches Volume 4*, Amsterdam, 1988, pages 21–40.
Robin Birley, 'Vindolanda' in *Current Archaeology* 116, London, August 1989, pages 275–9.
Robin Birley, 'Vindolanda' in *Current Archaeology* 128, London, March 1992, pages 344–9.
George C. Boon, *Isca: The Roman Legionary Fortress at Caerleon, Mon.*, Cardiff, 1972.
Alan K. Bowman, *Life and Letters on the Roman Frontier*, London, 1994.
Alan K. Bowman, 'The military occupation of Upper Egypt in the reign of Diocletian', *Bulletin of the American Society of Papyrologists* 15, 1978, pages 25–38.
Alan K. Bowman and J. David Thomas, 'A Military Strength Report From Vindolanda' in *JRS* 81, London, 1991, pages 15–26.
David Breeze, 'Demand and Supply on the Northern Frontier' in Roger Miket and Colin Burgess [edd.], *Between and Beyond the Walls: Essays on the Prehistory and History of North Britain in Honour of George Jobey*, Edinburgh, 1984, pages 264–286.
David J. Breeze and Brian Dobson, 'Fort Types as a Guide to Garrisons: A Reconsideration' in Eric Birley, Brian Dobson and Michael Jarrett, *Roman Frontier Studies 1969*, Cardiff, 1974, pages 13–19.
David J. Breeze and Brian Dobson, *Hadrian's Wall*, London, 1976.
David J. Breeze and Brian Dobson, 'Roman Military Deployment in North England' in *Britannia* 16, London, 1985, pages 1–19.
Andrew Burnett, 'Clipped Siliquae and the end of Roman Britain' in *Britannia* 15, London, 1984, pages 163–8.
Caesar, *de bello Gallico*.
Averil Cameron, *The Later Roman Empire AD 284–430*, London, 1993.
Brian Campbell, 'The Marriage of Soldiers under the Empire' in *JRS* 68, London, 1978, pages 153–166.
John Casey, *The Legions in the Later Roman Empire: The Fourth Annual Caerleon Lecture*, Caerleon, 1991.

P.J. Casey, 'The coins from the excavations at High Rochester in 1852 and 1855' in *Archaeologia Aeliana* 5th Series, Volume 8 (1980), pages 75–87.

P.J. Casey, 'The end of garrisons on Hadrian's Wall: an historico–environmental model' in *Bulletin of the London University Institute of Archaeology*, 1993, pages 69–80.

P.J. Casey, 'A Fifth Century Gallo–Roman Gold Coin from Piercebridge, County Durham' in *Durham Archaeological Journal* Volume 3, 1987, pages 5–7.

P.J. Casey, 'Magnus Maximus in Britain' in *The End of Roman Britain* BAR British Series 71, Oxford, 1979, pages 66–79.

P.J. Casey, *Roman Coinage in Britain*, Aylesbury, 1980.

P.J. Casey and J.L. Davies with J. Evans, *Excavations at Segontium (Caernarfon) Roman Fort, 1975–1979*, CBA Report 90, London, 1993.

G.L. Cheesman, *The Auxilia of the Roman Imperial Army*, Oxford, 1914.

Niketas Choniates, *O City of Byzantium*.

Claudian, *De Bello Getico*.

Claudian, *In Gildonem*.

Claudian, *On the Consulship of Stilicho*.

R.G. Collingwood and R.P. Wright, *The Roman Inscriptions of Britain, I Inscriptions on Stone*, Oxford, 1965.

Constantius, *Vita Germani*.

Corpus Inscriptionum Latinarum, Berlin, 1862–.

Cyril of Scythopolis, *Vita Sabae*.

C. Daniels 'Excavation at Wallsend and the fourth–century Barracks on Hadrian's Wall' in W.S. Hanson and L.J.F. Keppie [edd.], *Twelfth Congress of Roman Frontier Studies*, BAR S71, Oxford, 1980, pages 173–193.

K.R. Dark, 'A Sub–Roman Re–Defence of Hadrian's Wall?' in *Britannia* 23, London, 1992, pages 111–120.

Jeffrey L. Davies, 'Roman military deployment in Wales and the Marches from Pius to Theodosius' in Valerie A. Maxfield and Michael J. Dobson [edd.], *Roman Frontier Studies 1989*, Exeter, 1992, pages 52–57.

Jeffrey L. Davies, 'Soldiers, peasants and markets in Wales and the Marches' in T.F.C. Blagg and A.C. King [edd.], *Military and Civilian in Roman Britain*, BAR British Series 136, Oxford, 1984, pages 93–127.

R.W. Davies, 'Cohortes Equitatae' in *Historia*, Band 20, Wiesbaden, 1971.

R.W. Davies, 'The Supply of Animals to the Roman Army and the Remount System', *Latomus* Tome 28, Brussels, 1969, pages 429–59.

David P. Davison, *The Barracks of the Roman Army from the 1st to 3rd Centuries AD*, BAR International Series 472, Oxford, 1989.

George T. Dennis [tr.], 'The Anonymous Byzantine Treatise On Strategy' in *Three Byzantine Military Treatises: Dumbarton Oaks Texts No. IX*, Washington, D.C., 1985.

H. Dessau, *Inscriptiones Latinae Selectae*, Berlin, 1892–1916.

Geoffroy de Villehardouin, *Conquest of Constantinople*.

Karen R. Dixon and Pat Southern, *The Roman Cavalry: From the First to the Third Century AD*, London, 1992.

Dr Brian Dobson, 'The Empire' in *Warfare in the Ancient World*, edited by General Sir John Hackett, London, 1989, pages 192–221.

Michael H. Dodgeon and Samuel N.C. Lieu [edd.], *The Roman Eastern Frontier and the Persian Wars AD 226–363: A Documentary History*, London and New York, 1991.

J.N. Dore and J.P. Gillam, *The Roman Fort at South Shields: Excavations 1875–1975*, The Society of Antiquaries of Newcastle upon Tyne Monograph Series No. 1, Newcastle, 1979,

R.P. Duncan–Jones, 'The Choenix, the Artaba and the Modius,' *Zeitschrift für Papyrologie und Epigraphik* Band 21 (1976), Bonn, pages 43–52.

R.P. Duncan–Jones, 'Pay and Numbers in Diocletian's Army', *Chiron*, Band 8 (1978), München, pages 541–60. A revised version was published as chapter 7 of Richard Duncan–Jones's *Structure and Scale in the Roman Economy*, Cambridge, 1990, pages 105–17.

John R. Elting, *The Battle of Bunker's Hill*, Monmouth Beach, New Jersey, 1975.

Donald W. Engels, *Alexander the Great and the Logistics of the Macedonian Army*, Berkeley, 1978.

Ephemeris Epigraphica, Rome–Berlin, 1872–.

Simon Esmonde Cleary, 'Constantine I to Constantine III' in Malcolm Todd (ed.), *Research on Roman Britain: 1960–89*, Britannia Monograph Series No. 11, London, 1989, pages 235–244.

A.S. Esmonde Cleary, *The Ending of Roman Britain*, London, 1989.

Eugippius, *Vita Severini*.

Jeremy Evans, 'Settlement and Society in North England in the Fourth Century' in P.R. Wilson, R.F.J. Jones and D.M. Evans [edd.], *Settlement and Society in the Roman North*, Bradford, 1984, pages 43–48.

Robert O. Fink, 'Hunt's *Pridianum*: British Museum Papyrus 2851' in *JRS* 48, London, 1958 pages 102–116.

Robert O. Fink. *Roman Military Records on Papyrus* (Philological Monographs of the American Philological Association No. 26), Cleveland, Ohio, 1971 [=*RMR*].

D.J.V. Fisher, *The Anglo–Saxon Age c. 400–1042*, Harlow, 1973.

R.I. Frank, 'Scholae Palatinae: The Palace Guards of the Later Roman Empire' in *Papers and Monographs of the American Academy in Rome* 23 (1969), Rome.

D.H. French and C.S. Lightfoot [edd.], *The Eastern Frontiers of the Roman Empire*, BAR International

Series 553, Oxford, 1989.
Sheppard Frere, *Britannia*, London, 1967.
Nicholas Fuentes, 'Fresh thoughts on the Saxon Shore' in Valerie A. Maxfield and Michael J. Dobson [edd.], *Roman Frontier Studies 1989*, Exeter, 1992 pages 58–64.
Michael Fulford, 'The Economy of Roman Britain' in Malcolm Todd (ed.), *Research on Roman Britain: 1960–89*, Britannia Monograph Series No. 11, London, 1989, pages 175–201.
Gildas, *De Excidio Britonum*.
J.F. Gilliam, 'The Moesian "Pridianum"' in *Homages à Albert Grenier*, Brussels, 1962, pages 747–756.
R. Goodburn and P. Bartholomew, *Aspects of the* Notitia Dignitatum, BAR Supplementary Series 15, Oxford, 1976.
Pope Gregory I, *Epistulae*.
B.P. Grenfell, A.S. Hunt et alia [edd.], *The Oxyrhynchus Papyri*, London, 1898–.
Robert Grigg, 'Inconsistency and Lassitude: The Shield Emblems of the Notitia Dignitatum', *Journal of Roman Studies* 73, 1983, pages 132–142.
W.S. Hanson and D.B. Campbell, 'The Brigantes: from Clientage to Conquest' in *Britannia* 17, London, 1986, pages 73–89.
Mark Hassall, 'The Internal Planning of Roman Auxiliary Forts' in Brian Hartley and John Wacher, *Rome and Her Northern Provinces*, Gloucester, 1983, pages 96–131.
Peter Heather and John Matthews, *The Goths in the Fourth Century*, Translated Texts for Historians Volume 11, Liverpool, 1991.
Nicholas Higham, *Rome, Britain and the Anglo-Saxons*, London, 1992.
Nicholas Hodgson, 'The Notitia Dignitatum and the later Roman garrison of Britain' in Valerie A. Maxfield and Michael J. Dobson, *Roman Frontier Studies 1989: Proceedings of the XVth International Congress of Roman Frontier Studies*, Exeter, 1991, pages 84–92.
Dietrich Hoffmann, *Das Spätrömische Bewegungsheer und die Notitia Dignitatum*, Epigraphische Studien Band 7/1, Düsseldorf, 1969.
Dietrich Hoffmann, 'Die spätrömischen Soldatengrabschriften von Concordia' in *Museum Helveticum* 20 (1963), Basle/Stuttgart.
P. A. Holder, *The Roman Army in Britain*, London, 1982.
Paul A. Holder, *Studies in the Auxilia of the Roman Army from Augustus to Trajan*, BAR International Series 70, Oxford, 1980.
Horace, *Ars Poetica*.
A.S. Hunt and C.C. Edgar [edd.], *Select Papyri*, London, 1963.
'Hyginus', *de metatione castrorum*.
Ann Hyland, *Equus: The Horse in the Roman World*, London, 1990.
The International Institute for Strategic Studies, *The Military Balance 1993–1994*, London, 1993.
Benjamin Isaac, *The Limits of Empire: The Roman Army in the East*, Oxford, revised edition, 1992.
Benjamin Isaac, 'The Meaning of The Terms Limes and Limitanei' in *J.R.S.*, 78, London, 1988, pages 125–147.
Simon James, 'Britain and the Late Roman Army' in T.F.C. Blagg and A.C. King [edd.], *Military and Civilian in Roman Britain*, BAR British Series 136, Oxford, 1984, Chapter 7 (pages 161–186).
St. Jerome, *contra Iohannem Hierosolymitanum episcopum*.
Stephen Johnson, *Hadrian's Wall*, London, 1989.
Stephen Johnson, *Later Roman Britain*, London, 1980.
Stephen Johnson, *The Roman Forts of the Saxon Shore*, London, 1976.
A.H.M. Jones, *The Decline of the Ancient World*, London, 1966.
A.H.M. Jones, *The Later Roman Empire 284–602: A Social, Economic and Administrative Survey*, Oxford, 1964.
A.H.M. Jones, J.R. Martindale and J. Morris [edd.], *Prosopography of the Later Roman Empire* Volume 1, Cambridge, 1971.
Barri Jones & David Mattingly, *An Atlas of Roman Britain*, London, 1990.
R.F.J. Jones, 'Change on the Frontier: Northern Britain in the Third Century' in Anthony King and Martin Henig [edd.], *The Roman West in the Third Century: Contributions from Archaeology and History*, BAR International Series 109 (i), Oxford, 1981, pages 393–414.
Jordanes, *The Gothic History*.
Josephus, *Bellum Iudaicum*.
Julian, *Letter to the Athenians*.
David Kennedy, 'The Composition of a Military Work Party in Roman Egypt (*ILS* 2483: Coptos)' in *The Journal of Egyptian Archaeology* 71, 1985, pages 156–160.
David Kennedy, 'The East' in John Wacher (ed.), *The Roman World*, London, 1987, pages 266–300.
David Kennedy, 'Milliary Cohorts: The Evidence of Josephus, BJ III, 4, 2 (67) and of Epigraphy' in *Zeitschrift für Papyrologie und Epigraphik*, Band 50, Bonn, 1983, pages 253–263.
David Kennedy and Derrick Riley, *Rome's Desert Frontier: From the Air* London, 1990.
J.P.C. Kent, 'Coin evidence for the abandonment of a frontier province' in Erich Swoboda [ed.], *Carnuntina*, Graz, 1956, pages 85–90.
J.P.C. Kent, 'The end of Roman Britain: The Literary and Numismatic Evidence Reviewed' in P.J. Casey (ed.), *The End of Roman Britain*, BAR British Series 71, Oxford, 1979, pages 15–27.
Lawrence Keppie, *The Making of the Roman Army: From Republic to Empire*, London, 1984.
Anthony King and Martin Henig [edd.], *The Roman West in the Third Century: Contributions from Archaeology and History*, BAR International Series 109 (i), Oxford, 1981.
C.J. Kraemer, Jr., 'Non-literary Papyri' in *Excavations at Nessana, conducted by H.D. Colt, Jr.* Vol. 3,

Princeton, 1958.

[Lucius Caecilius Firmianus] Lactantius, *De Mortibus Persecutorum*, edited and translated by J.L. Creed, Oxford, 1984.

Michael Lapidge, 'Gildas's Education and the Latin Culture of Sub-Roman Britain' in Michael Lapidge and David Dumville [edd.], *Gildas: New Approaches to Studies in Celtic History V*, Woodbridge, 1984, pages 27–50.

Yann le Bohec, *The Imperial Roman Army*, London, 1994 [originally published as *L'Armée Romaine sous le Haut-Empire*, 1989].

Naphtali Lewis and Meyer Reinhold [edd.], *Roman Civilization Sourcebook II: The Empire*, New York, 1955.

Libanius, *Orationes*.

J.H.G.W. Liebeschuetz, *Barbarians and Bishops: Army, Church, and State in the Age of Arcadius and Chrysostom*, Oxford, 1990.

J.H.G.W. Liebeschuetz, 'Generals, Federates and Bucellarii in Roman Armies Around AD 400' in Philip Freeman and David Kennedy [edd.], *The Defence of the Roman and Byzantine East: Proceedings of a Colloquium held at the University of Sheffield in April 1986*, BAR International Series 297, Oxford, 1986, pages 463–474, reprinted in *From Diocletian to the Arab Conquest: Change in the Late Roman Empire*, Aldershot, 1990 (19).

Wolfgang Liebeschuetz, 'The end of the Roman army in the western empire' in John Rich and Graham Shipley [edd.], *War and Society in the Roman World*, Leicester-Nottingham Studies in Ancient Society Volume 5, London, 1993, pages 265–276.

Livy, *Ab urbe condita*.

John Lydus, *De Magistratibus (On Powers)*.

John Lydus, *De Mensibus*.

Ramsay MacMullen, 'How Big was the Roman Imperial Army?', *Klio*, Band 62 (1980), Berlin, pages 451–460.

Ramsay MacMullen, *Soldier and Civilian in the Later Roman Empire*, Cambridge, Mass., 1963.

John Malalas, *Chronographia [World Chronicle]*.

J.C. Mann, 'Birdoswald to Ravenglass', *Britannia* 20, London, 1989, pages 75–9.

J.C. Mann, 'The historical development of the Saxon Shore' in Valerie A Maxfield (ed.), *The Saxon Shore: A Handbook*, Exeter Studies in History No. 25, Exeter, 1989.

J.C. Mann, *Legionary Recruitment and Veteran Settlement during the Principate*, Insitute of Archaeology Occasional Publications No. 7, London, 1983.

J.C. Mann, 'Power, Force and the Frontiers of the Empire' in *J.R.S.*, 69, London, 1979, pages 175–183.

Robert Marichal, 'Les Ostraca de Bu Njem' in *Comptes Rendus de l'Academie des Inscriptions & Belles-Lettres*, 1979, pages 436–452.

J.R. Martindale (ed.), *Prosopography of the Later Roman Empire* Volume 2, Cambridge, 1980.

J. Maspéro, *Catalogue générale des antiquités égyptiennes du Musée de Caire; Papyrus grecs d'époque byzantine*, Cairo, 1911–16.

Valerie A. Maxfield and Michael J. Dobson [edd.], *Roman Frontier Studies 1989: Proceedings of the XVth International Congress of Roman Frontier Studies*, Exeter, 1991.

Mike McCarthy, Ian Caruana and Graham Keevill, 'Carlisle' in *Current Archaeology* 116 (August 1989), pages 298–302.

E. Nischer, 'The Army Reforms of Diocletian and Constantine and their modifications up to the time of the Notitia Dignitatum' in *J.R.S.*, 13, London, 1923.

Orosius, *Historia contra paganos*.

H.M.D. Parker, 'The Legions of Diocletian and Constantine' in *J.R.S.* 23, London, 1933, pages 175–189.

S. Thomas Parker, 'New Light on the Roman Frontier in Arabia' in H Vetters & M Kandler [edd], *Akten des 14. Internationalen Limeskongresses 1986 in Carnuntum*, Teil 1, Wien, 1990, pages 215–230.

S. Thomas Parker (ed.), 'The Roman Frontier in Central Jordan: Interim Report on the *Limes Arabicus* Project, 1980–1985' in BAR International Series 340, Oxford, 1987.

Pliny, *Letters*.

A Poidebard, *La trace de Rome dans le désert de Syrie*, 1934.

A. Poidebard and R Mouterde, *Le Limes de Chalcis*, 1945.

Polybius, *Histories*.

Procopius, *Aedificia*.

Procopius, *Anecdota*.

Procopius, *Bellum Gothicum*.

Procopius, *De Bello Persico*.

Procopius, *Vandal War*.

John Rich and Graham Shipley [edd.], *War and Society in the Roman World*, Leicester-Nottingham Studies in Ancient Society Volume 5, London, 1993.

I.A. Richmond, 'Roman Britain and Roman Military Antiquities' in *Proceedings of the British Academy*, 1955, pages 297–315.

A.L.F. Rivet and Colin Smith, *The Place-Names of Roman Britain*, London, 1979.

Margaret Roxan, 'Pre-Severan Auxilia Named in the Notitia Dignitatum' in R. Goodburn and P. Bartholomew [edd.], *Aspects of the **Notitia Dignitatum*** BAR Supplementary Series 15, Oxford, 1976.

Margaret Roxan, 'Women on the Frontiers' in Valerie A. Maxfield and Michael J. Dobson, *Roman Frontier Studies 1989: Proceedings of the XVth International Congress of Roman Frontier Studies*, Exeter, 1991, pages 462–7.

Peter Salway, *Roman Britain*, The Oxford History of England 1A, Oxford, 1981.

Scriptores Historiae Augustae.

C. Scorpan, *Limes Scythiae: Topographical and stratigraphical research on the late Roman*

fortifications on the Lower Danube, BAR International Series 88, Oxford, 1980.
Otto Seeck [ed.], *Notitia Dignitatum (omnium, tam civilium quam militarium, in partibus Orientis et in partibus Occidentis) accedunt Notitia Urbis Constantinopolitanae Provinciarum*, Berlin, 1876 [= N.D.].
J.C. Shelton, 'Two notes on the artab' in *Zeitschrift für Papyrologie und Epigraphik* Band 42 (1981), Bonn, pages 99–106.
T.C. Skeat (ed.), *Papyri from Panopolis: In The Chester Beatty Library Dublin*, Chester Beatty Monographs No. 10, Dublin, 1964.
C. Sebastian Sommer, *The Military Vici in Roman Britain: Aspects of their Origins, their Locations and Layout, Administration, Function and End*, BAR British Series 129, Oxford, 1984.
P. Southern, 'The Numeri of the Roman Imperial Army', *Britannia* 20, London, 1989, pages 81–140.
M. Speidel, 'The Pay of the Auxilia' in *JRS* 63, London, 1973, pages 141–147, reprinted in M. Speidel, *Roman Army Studies*, Amsterdam, 1984, pages 83–89.
M. Speidel, 'The Roman Army In Arabia' in *Aufsteig und Niedergang der römischen Welt* Berlin, II, 8 (1977), pages 687–730 [reprinted as M. Speidel, *Roman Army Studies* Volume 1, Amsterdam, 1984, pages 229–272], pages 727–8 = 269–70.
M. Alexander Speidel, 'Roman Army Pay Scales' in *JRS* 82, London, 1992, pages 87–106.
M.P. Speidel, 'The Soldiers' Servants' in Valerie A. Maxfield and Michael J. Dobson, *Roman Frontier Studies 1989: Proceedings of the XVth International Congress of Roman Frontier Studies*, Exeter, 1991, page 477.
K. Strobel, *Untersuchungen zu den Dakerkriegen Trajans*, Bonn, 1984.
Ronald Syme, 'The Lower Danube under Trajan' in *JRS* 49, London, pages 26–33.
Synesius, *Constitutio*.
Synesius, *Letters*.
Synesius, *De Regno*.
Tacitus, *Historiae*.
Arnold Taylor, *Harlech Castle*, Cardiff, 1988.
Themistius, *Orations*.
Codex of Theodosius.
Theophylact Simocatta, *(Universal) History*, translated with introduction and notes as *The History of Theophylact Simocatta* by Michael & Mary Whitby, Oxford, 1986.
J.D. Thomas and R.W. Davies, 'A New Military Strength Report on Papyrus' in *JRS* 67, London, 1977, pages 50–61.
J.O. Tjäder, *Die nichtliterarischen lateinischen Papyri Italiens aus der Zeit 445–700*, Lund, 1955.
Malcolm Todd [ed.], *Research on Roman Britain: 1960–89*, Britannia Monograph Series No. 11, London, 1989.
Malcolm Todd, *Roman Britain 55 BC – AD 400*, Glasgow, 1981.
Roger Tomlin, 'The Army of the Late Empire' in John Wacher [ed.], *The Roman World*, London, 1987, pages 107–120.
Roger Tomlin, 'The Late-Roman Empire' in General Sir John Hackett (ed.), *Warfare in the Ancient World*, London, 1989.
Roger Tomlin, 'The Mobile Army' in Peter Connolly (ed.) *Greece and Rome at War*, London, 1981, pages 249–259.
Roger Tomlin, '*Seniores–Iuniores* in the Late-Roman Field Army', *American Journal of Philology* Vol. 93, 2, 1972, pages 253–278.
J.M.C. Toynbee, *Animals In Roman Life and Art*, London, 1973.
L. Várady, 'New Evidences on Some Problems of the Late Roman Military Organisation', *Acta Antiqua Academiae Scientiarium Hungaricae* Tomus 9, Budapest, 1961, pages 333–96.
Vegetius, *Epitoma rei militaris*.
Velleius (Paterculus), *Historia Romana*.
A. von Domaszewski, *Die Rangordnung des römisches Heeres*, Cologne, 1967.
G.R. Watson, *The Roman Soldier*, London, 1969.
Colin M. Wells, 'Where Did They Put the Horses? Cavalry Stables in the Early Empire,' *Limes: Akte des XI. Internationalen Limeskongresses*, Budapest, 1977, pages 659–65.
C.B. Welles, R.O. Fink and J.F. Gilliam, *The Excavations at Dura-Europos: Final Report V, Part 1. The Parchments and Papyri*, New Haven, 1959.
C. Wessely, *Studien zur Palaeographie und Papyruskunde*, Leipzig, 1901–.
Dick Whittaker, 'Landlords and warlords in the later Roman Empire' in John Rich and Graham Shipley [edd.], *War and Society in the Roman World*, Leicester-Nottingham Studies in Ancient Society Volume 5, London, 1993, pages 277–302.
J. J. Wilkes, 'Early fourth century rebuilding in Hadrian's Wall forts' in M.G. Jarrett and B. Dobson [edd.], *Britain and Rome*, Kendal, 1966, pages 114–138.
Stephen Williams, *Diocletian and the Roman Recovery*, London, 1985.
Tony Wilmott, 'Birdoswald' in *Current Archaeology* 112 (December 1988) page 158, and 116 (August 1989) pages 288–291.
G. Zereteli, O. Krueger and P. Jernstedt, *Papyri russischer under georgischer Sammlungen*, Tiflis, 1925–35.
Zosimus, *Nea Historia*.
Constantine Zuckerman, '*Legio V Macedonica* in Egypt: CPL 199 Revisited', *Tyche*, 3 (1988), pages 279–87.

www.ingramcontent.com/pod-product-compliance
Ingram Content Group UK Ltd.
Pitfield, Milton Keynes, MK11 3LW, UK
UKHW061213180426
11947UKWH00029B/2024